Living For So Much More

FINDING THE STRENGTH TO SOAR IN LIFE AGAINST THE ODDS

RICHARD AKUBUIRO

Copyright © 2019 by Richard Akubuiro.
All rights reserved.

Requests for information should be addressed to:
gospelfoundationinternational@gmail.com

This book, or parts thereof, may not be reproduced, stored in a retrieval system, or transmitted in any form or by any means, electronic, mechanical, photocopying, recording or otherwise, without the written permission of the publisher.

Published By: Achievers World Publishing

ISBN: 978-0-6486778-0-2 (paperback)
ISBN: 978-0-6486778-1-9 (ebook)

Scriptures quotations marked (NIV) are taken from the Holy Bible, New International Version®, NIV® Copyright © 1973, 1978, 1984, 2011 by Biblica, Inc.® Used by permission. All rights reserved worldwide

Scriptures quotations marked (KJV) are taken from the King James Version of the bible

Printed in Australia

FOREWARD

Do you occasionally feel as if you are living in obscurity and wonder if a dream you once had will ever come to fruition? Are you driven by and seek to understand the success elements that make some people stand out as they rise to unique challenges, understand their dreams and achieve their God-ordained goals?

This book is about Richard's life-defining moments and the ways these experiences have influenced and shaped his life. You will have a closer look at how he responded to the difficulties he met along his way but particularly how he used them to his advantage and build a bridge into his destiny.

One of Richard's goals about this book is to help you find the components inside of you that could be your own potential seed of success and greatness. His story traces a path through his life as a young man and examines his actions, ordeals, struggles, commitment to God and strivings to attain his purpose through divine providence. Richard gives his readers an insight into how God has shaped and moulded his character through his faith and unrelenting trust in Him.

What was it about Richard that made him believe the vision an unseen Father gave to him in his youth? What about his experience can spark a revival in you to hold tenaciously to God's word? What can make you grab hold and journey into "what eyes have not seen, what ears have not heard, and what has never entered into a man's heart, but has been revealed by the Spirit to you?"

Engage with Richard and be truly inspired.

Lakers Komaiya

"God has a unique purpose for everything and everyone He created, but we remain destitute until we discover what it takes to fulfill our destiny in Him. The discovery of "the eagle seed" in us, will enable us to find the vigor and vitality to soar in life irrespective of setbacks. The inspiring experiences Richard shared in this book will both encourage and challenge you to soar high in life. Living for so much more should be the crave of every child of God."

— **PAUL DANGTOUMDA. (Director of YWAM Nigeria)**

DEDICATION

This Book is Dedicated to God- My Heavenly Father in memory of my Father Mr. Ebenezer Akubuiro and Mother Mrs. Paulina Akubuiro, whose legacy of love and kindness still lives on in the vision of Gospel Foundation international

Table of Contents

Introduction 1

PART 1: LIVING REALITIES 6

Chapter One: My Treasured Heritage 7

    The Graceful Hands of the Grand Weaver 7

    Alive and Free 9

    A Miraculous Escape 11

    A Season of Peace and Restoration 15

    Precious Memories 16

    A Legacy of Faith 18

    Reflection 20

Chapter Two: A Season of New Beginnings 21

    In Search of Hope 26

    Moment of Divine Encounter 29

    Taking a Stand 31

    Reflection 34

Chapter Three: Love Awakening 35

    An Unfair Social Contract 35

    The Miracle of Love and Acceptance 39

The Test of Trust 40

　　When Love Finds You 42

　　Love that Leaves No Question 45

　　Reflection 48

PART 2: LIVING ON THE EDGE 50

Chapter Four: Pressing Forward In The Face Of Adversity 51

　　Japanese Scholarship Adventure 52

　　Rural and Rugged Adventures 57

　　Life-Shaping Word 59

　　Reflection 61

Chapter Five: Seasons of Unseen Struggles 62

　　The Power of Influence 62

　　Line in the Sand Moment 65

　　The Reality of the Fight 69

　　Treading on Dangerous Ground 70

　　The Battle in the Garden 72

　　Reflection 75

Chapter Six: Seasons of Stretching and Straightening 76

　　A Journey out of My Comfort Zone 76

　　The First Surprise 80

　　The Second Surprise 82

The Third Surprise 84

Reflection 85

PART 3: LIVING HOPE 86

Chapter Seven: Life More Abundantly 87

Rural, Raw and Rugged 87

Alive and Free in the Philippines 92

Dark Cloud Lifted in New Zealand 92

Hope in Papua New Guinea 94

Little Be It or Much 95

Reflection 96

Chapter Eight: A Compelling Vision 97

Finding My Place 98

Dreams Come True 103

Reflection 104

Chapter Nine: An Adventure Of A Lifetime 105

The Provision 106

Cabin 270 109

Second Missionary Adventure 111

Immeasurably More 112

My Utmost for His Highest 113

Reflection: 115

Chapter Ten: Living Courageously 116

Living Courage 117

Inspiring Courage 120

Reflection 124

Let Hope Arise 126

The Summary of the Vision of the Gospel Foundation International ... 129

INTRODUCTION

LIVING FOR SO MUCH MORE

One of the most spectacular displays of the grandeur and creativity of God is seen in the open ocean. From the heights of the swells to the rumbling sounds of the wind and waves, His beauty speaks volumes. Yet, as majestic as these are, they are little in comparison to His splendour that lies below that deep blue sea.

Onboard the MV Doulos ship, on a voyage from the Philippines to Taiwan on the Western Pacific Ocean, we came a few hundred nautical miles near the Mariana Trench, the deepest known part of the ocean. The most memorable moment of that voyage was my time on the captain's deck, as we cruised along the calm seas and I imagined the magnitude and the wonders of God's creation in those deepest places. I stood amazed and overwhelmed by the spectacular demonstration of God's handiwork in those deepest parts of our planet. As I reflected on God's grandeur, I could not but think about the depth of His love for even the least of us.

The sight of the vastness of the ocean beyond the horizon and the thought of the unseen depth below that blue surface reminded me of how little I am, but also how big our God is. This momentary glimpse of the grandeur of His works in creation was the challenge I needed to take the limits off what He can do in and with my life.

In every generation, some ordinary people have dared to live for more than the ordinary life, as they *"launch out into the deep"* with God. *"There is no pit so deep that God's love is not deeper still."* These were the words of Corrie Ten Boom, after surviving the cruel ordeal of the Holocaust. In the depth of her ordeal, she found the strength to look past the traumas she had endured and reached deeper to the divine ocean of God's love and forgiveness.

If you have ever dreamed of doing something "big" with your life, something more than the ordinary, yet you are unwilling to leave the convenience of your comfort zone, I guess that just makes you human. The compelling message of this book is that no matter where we are in our journey, we have an invitation from God to come on board for an adventure of a lifetime. As we courageously take those baby steps of faith at His command and dare to do business with Him in the deeper waters of life above the ordinary, we will meet Him on the victory side beyond the limitations of our fears.

God has created us for so much more. We have His invitation to step out of our boats for an adventure, in pursuit of higher heights of hope and deeper depths of His love, by faith in who He is and will always be. It's my desire that every reader will look through the stories and experiences shared in this book to see the daily reality of millions of poor and disadvantaged young people around the world, whose dreams, visions, and stories are never told. Many never make it to the printed pages, nonetheless, they are never forgotten in God's eternal scheme of things.

Irrespective of our race, beliefs, and the colour of our skin, we all generally desire the same things in life. Whether it is hope, meaning, fulfillment, love, respect, and freedom, something within us wants to truly live. We just need to live long enough to realize that the source of what we seek, that purpose and satisfaction is hardly found in ourselves.

This book is not an autobiography; I leave that to the high and lofty members of our society. However, it is written autobiographically, not because I am somebody important or know about something that anybody needs to hear, but more because these stories are real, alive, and capable of inspiring hope in many who can identify with my experiences. The transformational impact of the stories and lived experiences of everyday people speaks for itself. I am hopeful that this book will encourage you to also share lessons learned from your stories because there is someone out there waiting to be blessed by the life experiences God has trusted you with.

Growing up in Africa, I always thought there was more to life than what my senses could see, hear, feel, taste, and smell. I guess curiosity sets us on a journey with some life-changing discoveries along the way. Another reason for this book is simply to remind me and perhaps someone else, of the unseen hands of the grand weaver through the tapestry of our stories, lest we forget.

To the poor families with disabled children in the remote African villages and the teenagers in the slums of South East Asia, and those who drop out of school with dashed hopes of ever breaking free from the generational cycle of poverty, I am thinking about you as I write this book. I hope somehow a copy of it gets into your hands. It's my hope and prayer that this book will inspire many more stories of people rising, to step into their places in this life adventure that God has promised. May we live every day on purpose for His good pleasure.

> *"Now to Him who is able to do immeasurably more than all we ask or imagine, according to His power that is at work within us."*
>
> **— (Ephesians 3:20)**

> *"When He had stopped speaking, He said to Simon, launch out into the deep and let down your nets for a catch."*
>
> **— (Luke 5:4)**

PART 1

Living Realities

CHAPTER ONE

My Treasured Heritage

---o---

"Everyone's life is a testimony in the making."

— Dan Davidson

The Graceful Hands of the Grand Weaver

A single thread in a tapestry though its colour brightly shines, can never see its purpose in the pattern of the grand design. And the stone that sits up on the very top of the mountains mighty face, does it think it's more important than the stones that form the base? So how can you see what your life is worth or where your value lies? You can never see through the eyes of man. You must look at your life through Heaven's eyes." - Lyrics of a soundtrack from The Prince of Egypt (Through Heaven's Eyes).

Coincidence can only be a lousy explanation when you consider the divine intelligence inter- woven in every cellular unit of our lives, and in the complexity of our individual experiences and stories. At the centre of all our stories with their ups and downs is the unseen hand of the grand weaver, diligently at work on the tapestry of our individual circumstances. He carefully weaves His way through the patterns, one thread at a time to make a beautiful masterpiece. Piece by piece, one experience after another, just like the grand weaver, God works behind the scenes of the seasons and events of our lives to make everything beautiful in His time. He patiently brings them all together including the grieves, the hurts, and the pains, as well as the joys. He fits them perfectly in harmony with His sovereign plans for our lives.

Here in retrospect, I will attempt to step back to trace some of the outstanding experiences of God's manifold grace, as He engineered the circumstances of my life and family to bring me right where I fitted in His strategic plan. As I write this book, one profound experience worth mentioning is the degree of freshness and clarity with which the memories of the events and stories I have written in these chapters came flowing through my mind. The details were as graphic as if they had just happened. In some instances, I could feel almost the same emotions associated with those experiences as real as they were when they actually occurred.

Alive and Free

God has helped me to experience healing where necessary. The healing process for some of the sad experiences took longer than others. Some of those agonizing events that impacted me most were the traumatic experiences my parents endured at the hands of militant Islamic Jihadists in Northern Nigeria. However, God has helped me come to the place of forgiveness. I have now experienced healing from the brokenness and heaviness in my heart, as well as the anger and resentment I once harboured for the perpetrators. I can boldly say that God has brought me to the place where I am keen to share His love with them in any way I can.

I share these stories as a tribute to God's faithfulness and in memory of my precious parents: Mr. Ebenezer and Mrs. Paulina Akubuiro who have both gone to be with the Lord in glory. In a sense, I consider my life one of their legacies. The pain they endured, the precious seeds they sowed into people's lives and their commitment to God are a big part of my treasured spiritual heritage.

"Before I formed you in the womb, I knew you."

— (Jeremiah 1:5 NIV)

The story of my family is certainly that of a grand demonstration of God's grace and mercy through a series of valleys and shadows of life experiences. It's little wonder they gave me the middle name Chidiebere, which in the Igbo language means "God is merciful."

Our family started relatively financially comfortable by Nigerian standards. My father was a pretty resilient and successful businessman who understood what it means to pick up the pieces from ground zero after a devastating storm of life. He was a godly man and a successful entrepreneur who loved God and was willing to serve Him as a tent-making missionary with his business platform. He loved people and cared for the poor and vulnerable members of our community.

After a devastating experience in the Northern part of Nigeria where they were serving the community in the then Adamawa province of North-eastern Nigeria as a lay missionary, he established a successful business. This placed him in an influential position to make a positive impact in the community. He supported the poor, disabled, and vulnerable people in society. He advocated for them and helped develop their capacities to support their families. He also created jobs for many of them in his business.

My father's genuine love for the people and his commitment to their welfare endeared my family to the local community. However, it didn't take too long for the religious hardliners of the majority Muslim North-eastern region to become envious and hostile. With the dawning of the Nigerian civil war in 1967, almost a decade before I was born, that hostility soon spiralled out of control. The Islamic Jihadist and the other extreme Islamic groups wasted no time in seizing the opportunity to wipe out the Christian community in the North-East. Unfortunately, more than fifty years afterward, the same radical Islamic spirit is still alive and very active in this geographical location in Nigeria. They are now known as Boko Haram.

A Miraculous Escape

The present Adamawa state located in the North-eastern part of Nigeria, which was then known as the Adamawa province was a thriving commercial centre of Northern Nigeria. My father had a thriving business trading quality fabric and textile material. His integrity, commitment to quality, and love for the local people soon earned him the respect of the business community and an open door for ministry among the local Hausa people.

In the lead up to the Nigerian civil war, hostility against Christians in the majority Muslim Northern Nigeria started to grow and gradually intensified. At this stage, my parents didn't have much to worry about as they had integrated well into their community and had become valuable community members, but even that was about to change.

As a little boy, I still remember the chilling feeling in my body when my Mum first told me the story of their ordeal that fateful day when those Jihadists had planned their destruction. A group of radical Muslims armed with every deadly and crude weapon imaginable surrounded their house chanting "Allahu Akbar." The series of events that followed this attack was worse than a horror movie. According to Mum, they did not see this coming. Weeks before this time, they had heard the rumours of Biafra separation from Nigeria and the possibility of armed conflict, but nothing too serious to start planning an escape at the time.

With absolutely no regard for human lives, this deadly mob invaded my family's home and looted everything they could find. They bundled up my entire family and literally threw them into a large pickup truck full of other people they had marked out for mass destruction and burial. In that dungeon of despair with certain death staring them in the face, Mum said all they could do was to look up to heaven from whence their only help could come. Then, they waited to take their last breath and appear in the presence of Jesus in glory. She said the condition in that death truck was unthinkable.

Guided by their local agents, these Jihadists were all over the community searching for Christians from home to home. The attack was relentless. They destroyed the Christians' homes and looted their properties in a calculated determination to completely wipe out any memories of them from that community. Churches were burnt down and businesses looted. This was the advent of a very sad and dark period for Nigeria and especially for the thriving province of Adamawa. It was the end of religious freedom as we know it in this part of Nigeria. Just like many original inhabitants of Northern Nigeria before the arrival of the Usman Dan-Fodio Jihad, this was a very gloomy and sorrowful time for all the Christians who called this province home. Many of whom are from the South-eastern part of the country.

Amid a hopeless situation, the light of God's mercy reached out to my family in an unexpected way. It came when the very hope of living was gone. As they waited in despair for their dying moments, for some reason one of the Jihadists in charge of the execution of the Christians, commanded one of their men to go and find out the number of people in the truck before they headed out to where they would kill them and dispose of their bodies.

Mum said they sat in the overcrowded pickup truck with their arms and legs tied with cords. As they prayed and hoped against hope, suddenly, the entrance latch to the pickup truck opened. Someone who looked a bit familiar to my parents was counting the heads of people who were alive on the truck. Out of the blue, he stopped counting when he drew near to them. He came closer and carefully observed the face of my Dad and Mum as if he knew them. And he whispered their names. It turned out that he was one of the local people my parents had helped. He was very sorry and could not stomach the and thought of killing a family that had shown him and his family so much love and kindness. He quickly ran off returned just as fast. He untied my family, hurried them out of the truck, and helped them escape. The journey from that death truck back to my village in Eastern Nigeria was literally through the valley of the shadow of death. But eventually, they made it back home alive.

The three years that followed were the darkest seasons in Nigerian history, with the breakout of the Nigerian Biafra war. For many families who originated from the Igbo ethnic group of South- eastern Nigeria, this was a very dark era. And it was even worse for the remnant of the Christian community in Northern Nigeria when the Biafra war raged from the 6th of July 1967 to the 15th of January 1970. It was a civil conflict that led to the loss of millions of precious lives.

A Season of Peace and Restoration

My parents made it home through the jungles, but they had to face the harsh realities of dealing with the loss of their home, business, livelihood, and all the material possessions they had accumulated over the years of living in Adamawa. Nevertheless, according to Mum, they found the strength in God to build again from nothing. After the Biafra war and living safely home in our village of Umudim in the South-East state of Imo, they began the long road of rebuilding their lives from ground zero.

After those three awful years of devastation of properties and the slaughter of millions of precious lives, the rage and hostility of the Biafra war subsided. The survivors worked hard as they tried to pick up the pieces of their broken lives. For some people like my parents who had lost everything, the recovery journey was an even longer one. The years that followed the war were tough, to say the least, but with God on their side, my father persevered and started a small building material business in the local village market known as Eke-Atta. This was about the time I came along in 1976.

Precious Memories

My memories of life at home in our village in my early years could be elusive, but a few events are still fresh in my mind as if they happened yesterday. I reflected on the time when our village had no electricity and tap water. To get water, we had to make a round trip about 40 kilometres to the nearest stream, which was the water source for the community. Unfortunately, not a lot has changed after many years. I remember the singing and dancing for joy in the community when high tension electric poles were erected in our village. The hope of getting electricity brought so much joy to the community. Dad was involved in the talks with the authorities regarding bringing electricity to our village. He raised our hopes as he spoke about the opportunities and developments that would come to the community once we had electricity.

I was particularly excited when he said he intended to get the electric power in our home and then he would buy a television. Just the prospect of having those things brought great happiness to my little heart. I trusted Dad's every word and knew he would come through. Television was a big deal for us kids. The village had just managed to collectively purchase a TV, and every child looked forward to going to the village hall to watch the shows. So, it was certainly a pleasant dream of having one at home. Unfortunately, we never quite got to own a TV in that village.

Dad prospered in his business and soon opened another business for Mum to manage. She was managing a stockfish business. Both businesses grew to the extent that our family enjoyed another season of financial blessings. As their businesses prospered so did their commitment to God in the local Anglican church and their ministry to the poor and vulnerable members of our community. Soon Dad bought a motorcycle, which is a big deal in a poor village. And afterward, he was about ready to buy a car, which, unfortunately, did not materialize in his lifetime.

In this season of prosperity, my family became a beacon of hope and help shining bright in the village. Dad came alongside families and supported them as they journeyed through the post-war rebuilding process. My family was again fully back in their usual business of loving, helping, and caring for the poor and the needy in the community. They did not only teach us kids these principles of love and care for others, but they exemplified it as a lifestyle. Dad demonstrated a lifestyle of servant leadership that everyone who knew him would testify of. This was in his DNA, and he passed it down to us as a heritage. This compassion and commitment to bringing help and hope in a very practical way, have inspired a vision of Gospel Foundation International (GFI).

A Legacy of Faith

I was very close to my father and still remember tagging along on the back of his bicycle and motorcycle on his way to the shop. As a toddler, a typical weekday routine in my family after getting out of bed would be to have our family devotions. After that, Dad would get ready to go to the shop, my siblings would prepare for school, Mum would get ready to go to the farm, and I would make preparations to go with Dad where ever he was going. I could tell he enjoyed having me around. He was very gracious with me when I got in the way or into stuff. I learned so much about the Father's heart of God by just observing Dad with my child's eyes. He consciously made efforts to point me to God.

I remember his regular scripture memorizing exercises. He made it so much fun to memorize the Bible. The rewards he gave motivated me to retain even more. I still have most of the Bible passages he helped me memorize alive in my memory today. One of my favourites is Romans Chapter 8. He was so pleased with me when I finally memorized the 39 verses of that Bible passage. Interestingly, I still have those 39 verses alive in my memory like a treasured heritage from him. This legacy for me is priceless and certainly a treasure I am very intentional about passing on to my kids.

These precious memories and stories of courage, perseverance, and the celebration of God's faithfulness through the darkest shadows of human experience to the sun-light paths of hope have become a treasured heritage for me. One of my motivations for writing this book is simply to remind myself, and maybe generations yet unborn, of the presence of the unseen hand of God available to help us in times of need, as evidenced in these stories. May the memories of God's help in the ages past reinforce hope in us for years to come. And may the remembrance of His saving grace through the valleys of our life experiences generate inner strength to stand, in the face of obstacles as we dare to live for so much more. Lest we forget.

My parents' legacy of care and compassion for the vulnerable members of our communities has inspired the Gospel Foundation International Legacy Project. A bit more about this vision is briefly explained on the last page of this book and the full details is available upon request.

Reflection

"Happy is He who has the God of Jacob for his help, whose hope is in the Lord his God"

— (Psalm 146:5).

"What we are is God's gift to us; what we become is our gift to Him."

— Louis Nizers

CHAPTER TWO

A Season of New Beginnings

"Even though I walk through the darkest valley, I will fear no evil"

— (Psalm23:4).

Storytelling was a great part of growing up and an important way of passing down traditions and cultural identities from one generation to another. We spent time after dinner in different age groups listening to tales and folklore. I still remember recreating pictures of those stories in my mind. Many of our cultural values and traditions were communicated through them. That being said, just as good tools can be used for evil purposes, these myths and legends are also instrumental in reinforcing the strongholds of fear and limitations for many of us.

As I was growing up, I noticed an increased awareness of the spiritual realm and a strong fear of the powers of darkness. As the years went by, my path crossed some people who had strange connections with the spirit world, and I saw the troubles that connection brought to them and their families. Consequently, I resolved in my heart not to have anything to do with the spirit world. I was determined to stay clear of anything that had to do with the dark world out of fear for my future and wellbeing. Growing up in a Christian family, I knew about the power of God but didn't think God was personal enough to step into the issues of my personal life. So I didn't worry much about seeking Him as a way of dealing with my fear of evil and the dark world.

A Fight with Fear

As a child, I enjoyed learning to read and write at home while looking forward to my 6th birthday when I would become eligible to enrol at the local primary school. I dreamed about wearing the white and blue community school uniform. For some reason, I considered the uniform to be prestigious at the time. It wasn't too long before I finally achieved what I longed for. Soon I was wearing my own white and blue school uniform and walking the 19-kilometre dirt road to school with the rest of the kids in the community. It was a daily excitement to join the group of kids in the neighbourhood early in the morning to take that long trek to school. The group walk to school was always fun and something to look forward to. But the walk back home from school was always the difficult part. It was hot. We would trudge the long road through the heat of the day, with average temperatures in the mid-thirty degrees centigrade and high humidity. In addition to the hot temperatures and humidity, we had the hot soil under our feet to deal with. For many of the kids without any footwear, the only hope of reprieve from the sun-heated ground beneath us was the shade from the trees along the way. Sadly, after all these years, this is still the daily reality for many kids in some countries including Nigeria.

I settled into my school routine and made it through to the third year. But sure enough, I noticed an adversary among the kids. I called him an adversary because he introduced himself to me as such. On one of those hot days after school, as we walked home in a rather smaller group than usual, I saw this tall and lanky boy with a mean look on his face in the group. For some reason, he was known as "Bomboy." He happened to have moved from another school to my school and lived a few kilometres away from us. He was not very bright in class but found absolute delight in harassing and tormenting the other kids.

I found out later that Bomboy's bullying disposition was a spill over from his troubled upbringing and family experiences. Even though Bomboy was not very smart, he certainly was skilful in his mastery of the act of bullying. Fear has a crippling hold on its victims, and this gave strength to the bullying. This was the strategy Bomboy used on the other kids. He particularly picked on me and made life unbearable for other kids. The fun of going home from school in a group was lost from the moment Bomboy turned up. Before long, he subtly demanded the respect of the kids through horror stories of his grandmother's spiritual adventures with the marine spirit. I remember some of his gruesome stories about his grandmother sacrificing one of her newborn babies at the shrine of an evil spirit. As expected, the purpose of these stories was to instil fear in the hearts of the kids, so no one would dare to challenge him. Apparently, he accomplished that for a time. It didn't take him too long to intimidate all the kids into obeying whatever he said.

Once he established his bullying influence over the kids, Bomboy was ready to unleash his other tactics. These came in various forms. Sometimes, he would demand one of the kids to bring snacks or fruit from home for him. Other times, he would demand that someone surrendered their lunch to him and other very random requests. With each bullying tactic he pulled, he would make you remember the consequences of non-compliance or telling adults what he was doing. He would report you to his Grandmother who would straighten you out on her spiritual altar.

For many kids like me who did not wish to mess with the dark spiritual world, our only option was full cooperation.

Sadly, not much has changed when it comes to bullying today. Even though the forms and strategies may be different, the connection to the spirit of fear is the same in spite of the time, location, and age. I remember having thoughts about taking on Bomboy in a fight or even reporting him to the teachers at school or my family members at home. But I never did. However, it was not too long before relief came to the kids, especially all his victims. Bomboy dropped out of school.

Every victory over bullying in its varying forms first comes from standing up to the spirit of fear. At that stage in my life, I didn't think I could break free from the stronghold of fear. Even after Bomboy was out of the picture, for many years I still had to deal with the impact of those seeds of fear in my life, until I experienced personal freedom in Christ. It certainly makes sense to me when the Bible speaks about God not giving us the spirit of fear.

"For God has not given us the spirit of fear, but of power and of love and of a sound mind"

— (2 Timothy 1:7).

I've heard stories of bullies like Bomboy who were defeated when victims stood up to them, bringing to an end their cruel and unkind acts. However, like many young people, especially those who are currently enduring bullying, I know there is an unwillingness to take on the bully physically because of the spiritual fear factor. I also considered the temporary measure of avoiding him as much as possible as a quick way out, but we know how ineffective that approach can be.

What was interesting though, was how this bullying adversity all ended. The trouble was the entire bullying experience opened up doors for the spirit of fear in my life. And I think it was this fear that challenged me to start looking for help. I am thankful that I found that victory over the spirit of fear in the triumph of Jesus Christ over the power of death and hell. There you go! What the Enemy intended for evil, God used for my good.

In Search of Hope

By this time, I had heard enough about the message of God's love for me to know that my help could come from Him, but I was not quite sure how to find Him. I knew some very nice people who are practicing Christians in the village, but most of them were older just like my Mum, and it didn't sound fashionable hanging out with a bunch of old folks in fellowship. I never thought young people could successfully follow Jesus at that prime of their lives in our world as it is today.

From up close, I observed the lives of some of my school mates and relatives who had personal relationships with God, and I desired what they had. However, at that time in my life, I had already immersed myself in the pursuit of teenage lust. I was beginning to earn the respect and envy of my peers. In my little way, I was progressively expanding my sphere of influence. My friends thought I had things going for me, but I knew better than that. In many ways, my actions were stumbling blocks to my true inner desires and search for meaning in my life. What

I truly desired was a personal and real relationship with God but had no idea how that could be possible. On the other hand, I was sure that the news of my conversion to a believer and follower of Jesus Christ would not go down well with my circle of friends and admirers.

I knew there was a God-shaped hole in my heart that nothing and no one but Him could fill. I knew I needed the Saviour. It was a season of searching for life's meaning among my circle of friends. One of my friends and relative became a Christian about this same period. I observed the sudden but undeniable transformation in his life and character for the better. I witnessed a genuine change in everything about him, so much so that I became very curious to know what had happened. Chibuzo was very happy to share his new-found faith in Jesus Christ and how he came to commit his life and future into God's hands. His explanation did not appeal to my logical and scientific mind, but the evidence in his life and character was compelling.

My initial response was to make fun of him, but as I carefully observed the transformation of character and genuine changes that had taken place in his life and relationships, I knew only God could have done that in his life. It was as if the whole message of the good news of God's love and grace was beginning to make sense. Chibuzor's life-transforming encounter with Jesus simplified the gospel to me. I saw that God is still in the business of saving lives and giving people new beginnings. And I wanted one. I wanted Him to touch my heart, just as pure and genuine as he did in the life of my cousin. This soon became my prayer every day as much as I could remember. God will always hear when anyone calls out to Him in truth and with expectation, and that included me.

"For everyone who calls on the name of the Lord will be saved."

— (Romans 10:13 NIV)

Moment of Divine Encounter

In the second year of secondary school or the equivalent of year eight, my heart was reaching out more and more for God, but I was still not ready to take that step towards God's waiting arms. But little did I know that all along, God's waiting arms were reaching out to me. There was a Scripture Union Student's Fellowship meeting in my school every Thursday afternoon after school. I had never bothered to find out what in the world those students did inside that classroom. But that afternoon, I sneaked out of the company of my usual circle of friends to attend. Nothing much changed in my life that day, but I felt a sense of peace and joy in the company of the students in the meeting that inspired me to go again.

That first day became the first of many. Then my moment of encounter with God came on one of the days when the student's fellowship had a visit from one of their senior friends who shared very clearly about God's love and His plan of salvation that took Jesus to the cross. In a very simple way, the message of God's love was explained from the gospel of John 3:16: *"For God so loved the world that He gave His only begotten Son, that whoever believes in Him, should not perish but have everlasting life."* What still stands out for me at that moment is the fact that I am loved and valued by God and that He would go all the way to that cruel cross to prove it. I imagined that if I was the only person on earth, Jesus would still go to the cross for me.

I felt an overwhelming sense of God's love and presence that dissolved my fears and doubts. God's love became so real to me, and I wondered why I had not spent every moment of my life since I was born living for Him. All I wanted to do was worship Him and live every moment loving and living as He would.

What I will forever remember about that precious moment, was the burning desire in my heart to love and worship God with everything within me for all eternity. I felt God's love in a measure that is hard to describe. The second thing that is etched in my memory is the inner strength I had to pursue God and the joy of doing so. I was in no illusion that it would be an easy road, but I knew that it would never be a lonely one. I had the assurance of God's presence through the seasons of life and in eternity.

At that moment of leaning into God's love, I went to Him just as I was, and prayed from my heart to Him. This was not about religion for me; it was real life. I was not there to join the Christian religion but to experience life. In John 10:10, Jesus made a very bold claim. He said, *"I have come that they may have life in abundance."* I went in search of this life that Jesus promised. I saw it at work in my cousin's life, so I knew it was real. I left that place with absolute assurance that God heard my prayer, and He certainly began a good work in my life. I knew that I had found my place in God's family, and nothing could separate me from my Father's love.

The experience of that moment was as simple and authentic as life itself. I felt as if I had made a transaction with God, and He was waiting for that moment my entire life. This new-found personal assurance of God's love awakened a natural love for Him and the things He cares about.

Taking a Stand

It was not long before my friends heard the rumours of my new-found faith; they wanted to find out for themselves. I was delighted to share my experience with God with anyone in that classroom. Sure enough, all my friends came to hear my story. Some of them also wanted to know more about Jesus, while others did not believe me at first and set a date when I would return to my former way of life. I wish I could say that those early years were all a smooth ride from glory to glory. Unfortunately, the reality is that authentic spiritual growth happens in the face of real-life challenges.

I had a childhood friend named KC who was notorious and very trendy. He was skilful in the act of adolescent mischief. He was once a fierce rival in all sorts of youthful and adolescent mischievous adventures. We competed for the most attention of the beautiful girls around and made up stories that would make them think we were the coolest guys in town. It was this boy who introduced me to the act of chasing girls. He seemed to know all the tricks in the book. The time came when I had to face him. I was not sure how that was going to work. I wondered what words I would even start with. How would I explain my new-found faith in Christ to KC? I thought I needed more time to prepare "my defence" before I eventually face him.

KC had moved to the city for school, and we would catch up occasionally when he visited the village. One of those Christmas seasons, I attended the traditional wedding ceremony of one of our relatives and was not expecting KC to be there. Unfortunately, there he was all over the place looking for me. I didn't feel prepared to face him. Yet, I knew if I didn't speak up to inform him about my faith, it may be too late by the time I let him tell me what was on his mind. I thought about what and how I could share my story with him but didn't feel courageous at all. I had a major struggle with my pride and was somewhat ashamed of Christ. For some reason, I decided that the smartest way to handle the situation was to deliberately avoid contact with him. So, I hid from him. I saw him in the midst of the crowd a few times and snuck away with my seat in a corner. The down-side of hiding out was that my back was against the wall, and that didn't give me many options for escape.

Sure enough, he found me. Apparently, he was asking around and someone had given him a hint where to find me. It was not long before I saw him wading through the crowd as he made his way to my direction. We made eye contact and, oops! It was too late for me to run. He flashed his mischievous smile as he charged for our usual hoodie handshake. At that moment, amidst the fierce battle, I found the inner strength to share about the work of grace God had started in my heart with my friend KC. I couldn't be any happier that I did.

As expected, he was a bit disappointed that I was not going to connect him to a particular girl he was after whom he reckoned was fond of me. I felt as if all of heaven was applauding me. I felt alive and believe me, that was a really good feeling.

Reflection

"If anyone is in Christ, he's a new creation, old things are passed away and all things have become new."

— (2 Corinthians 5:17)

"You have made us for Yourself, O Lord, and our heart is restless until it finds its rest in You."

— St. Augustine of Hippo.

CHAPTER THREE

Love Awakening

"Love in our hearts is God's potent tool to reach our broken world."

— Unknown

An Unfair Social Contract

"There is neither Jew nor Gentile, neither slave nor free, nor is there male and female, for you are all one in Christ Jesus." (Galatians 3:28)

The seasons of our lives are punctuated with the miracles of God's love. Many of which we let slip by without much thought and appreciation for their rare beauties. I mean, those special moments when the sweetness of God's love and grace break into our little world. Those of us who have experienced rejection at some point on our journey would appreciate the difference it makes in our lives when someone extends the hands of authentic love and acceptance. Sometimes it takes one act of genuine care and acceptance to mitigate the impact of years of rejection. You may not appreciate how much of a blessing it is to be accepted until you have experienced rejection.

"Birds of the same the feathers flock together." This is an Igbo adage that expresses some of the long-held traditions in Nigerian society, as well as many other cultures. The words of that adage are certainly true about the caste system in India, Nigeria, and many other countries. This unwritten social contract simply suggests that if you're from the lower class of society, you have no business mingling with the upper class. The social expectation is that you hang around those from your societal class. The system will not fail to call you to order if you choose to violate this socio-cultural norm.

Growing up in a lower economic class in Nigeria, I had no illusions about the limitations of the class in which I belonged. I accepted and was respectful of that. It was never my intention to rebel against those repressive social contracts. I completely understood my place in those unwritten caste rules. The system did not waste any time to "call me to order" when I attempted to push those boundaries. Naturally, friendships developed across the class divide with the potential of becoming more serious relationships, especially at the university. That is when the divide became even more evident for me.

Class Conflict

It was natural to deal with the fallout of the social segregation based on my family's social- economic status because I was not going to force myself into a place where I was not welcomed. I was content with my family's social status, even though I was not particularly happy with it. I was intentional about my determination to break free from that cycle of poverty. The low side of that social divide was not exactly a very pleasant one to belong to, especially when you are a leader with your team and friends on the elevated side of the divide.

An example of the conflict I faced as friendships naturally developed during my university years occurred when a friend of mine introduced his sister to me. In time, we become good friends as well. The major problem here was that they belonged to an upper-class family. Predictably, when the family saw the potential of a more serious relationship developing between their daughter and me, they held back no words or actions to remind me that I did not belong to their class, therefore I was not welcome in their family.

For many, such an experience would further deteriorate already fragile self-esteem and weaken struggling courage. The poor guy would be afraid to step out of his comfort zone. But again, it's not what happens to us that decides our fate, but our attitudes in life that make the difference. I could have chosen bitterness, but what difference would that make? I think I know better than that. I have learned that there is an appointment in every disappointment.

As sad as that season of my life was, I'm sure God used it to help me discover other aspects that needed some work, as well as areas of strength that required further nurturing. Ever since I became a Christian, I always sincerely sought God's help in prayer about who I should marry when the time was right. I also made a commitment to God that I would trust Him to guide me to the right girl I would spend the rest of my life with as my wife. I have always been very confident in God's ability to answer this life-long prayer of mine. Consequently, I have also always been careful when it comes to relationships with members of the opposite sex. I was very conscious about what I said and did, even more so because of my position as a leader among the students.

Richard Akubuiro

The Miracle of Love and Acceptance

Many years after those experiences with rejection, God was gracious enough to bring me to a different socio-cultural experience I never knew existed. Two years into my mission adventure with the MV Doulos in 2008, I met the most beautiful girl in the entire world who eventually became my wife. As our friendship and relationship grew, it became important for me to meet her parents in Western Australia. By this time, I was living in Papua New Guinea and Tracey was working with the Operation Mobilization team in Albania.

I had to make that journey down to Albany in Western Australia to meet her father by myself. As you can imagine, that took all the courage and strength I could gather, especially given my previous experience with rejection from that upper social-cultural class. I was not sure what to expect but was reassured by a deep-seated sense of peace in my heart. On arrival, I was treated as an honoured guest beyond anything I have ever experienced. The warmth, acceptance, and simplicity of their love for who I am, was like an ointment of healing for the past rejection I had encountered. This family taught me what it means to value people irrespective of the colour of their skin and their socio-economic class.

Then came the moment when I was going to officially ask Rev. Bill for his permission to marry his daughter Tracey. I had taken hours to rehearse my words and gather the courage to say what was on my mind as it was. I was extremely nervous and concerned that I would screw up an awesome relationship that was beginning to make the difference in my life. Again, I was wrong about the anticipated outcome. Contrary to my fears, I received my father-in-law's support to go ahead and formally propose to his daughter. I received the blessing for our marriage and a joyful welcome into the Byleveld family. What else could I ask for?

The Test of Trust

About a year after receiving my father-in-law's blessing, Tracey and I got married in Nigeria. After the wedding, we were ready to head back to Australia. Going through the immigration requirements for Australia, I was informed about the options of applying for a marriage visa onshore or offshore. My wife and I decided that we would settle for the option of applying for the Australian marriage visa onshore, especially as I already had a valid Australian tourist visa in my passport, which needed to be used. Having considered this option, I booked a one-way flight from Lagos to Australia.

Everything as much as we know was fine until I was informed by the airline about two days before my travel, that I would not be allowed into the airplane if I didn't have a return ticket to Nigeria. That should not have been much of an issue as I had enough savings in an account in an Australian bank. I had been saving some money in my bank account in Australia as part of my plans to complete a master's degree program in that country. From that savings, I could have easily paid for this return ticket without stress. But the trouble was that I could not access my Australian bank account from Nigeria. I tried to look at other possible options including borrowing from friends and relatives, but it all came down to asking if my father-in-law could lend me the money for the ticket. I would refund him as soon as I had access to my account.

As much as I could remember, this was one of the most difficult decisions I have ever had to make. Very mindful of the odds against me as a Nigerian national, I have always been extremely careful not to give a reason for my integrity and authenticity to be questioned. This was one of those down moments. With my imagination gone wild, I could only dwell on what they would think about me. Furthermore, would they even believe that I was telling the truth? These thoughts reinforced my fears and reopened deep heart injuries inflicted by experiences of rejection. I was very worried about the concern or even the potential strain my request would put on my wife's relationship with her parents.

On the other side of the world down under, my parents-in-law understandably had their fears, but they loved and accepted me enough to face those concerns and dared to believe in me and my story. They sent me the money for the ticket, and everything went well as planned, but this single gesture of trust and acceptance did more than buying me a return ticket. It became one of God's prescriptions to completely heal me of the injuries inflicted by my experiences of rejection.

When Love Finds You

"Let the morning bring me word of your unfailing love, for I have put my trust in You. Show me the way I should go, for to You I entrust my life."

— (Psalm 143:8 NIV)

These words of the psalmist became the words of my prayers many years ago as I looked to God to help me in various areas of my life, especially in the area of marriage. As a young man, I have seen people make the wrong choices in fundamental aspects of their lives including marriage. Hence that prompted a deep concern that compelled me to seek God in prayer for help on my journey through those crucial junctions of life. I believe the decision about who to settle down with in marriage is very significant. Who you marry, is one of the most critical decisions you will ever make; thus, you should never take it lightly. Knowing this, I have purposefully prayed the words of David in Psalm 143:8.

As life happened, friendships developed, and I considered whether or not a particular girl was the right one for me I would pray that Psalm. Each time my heart drifted toward any girl I developed a liking for, as soon as I returned to my senses, the words of that scripture would again be the words of my heart's cry to God in prayer. I do not doubt that God is real enough to show up for my help in times of need. For me, it was very important that I get it right in marriage as I have seen too many people who stumbled at this stage in their lives.

When my relationship with my wife Tracey started growing. We were in love and things looked pretty good with the prospect of spending our lives together forever. However, I always knew when it was time to get back to my Psalm 143:8 prayer scripture.

I needed to get God's perspective on our relationship. I was sincerely looking up to God for clarity and assurance that I was on the right path. As I continued with this prayer, our love for each other grew even more. There was more mutual openness and vulnerability with each other, even with the vast geographical distance between us. Soon, we become best friends with complete transparency and deeply in love with each other.

I was still going back to Psalm 143:8 prayer because I was not sure if this growing love was God's answer. I needed more assurance or confirmation than that. I also needed God to try my heart and deal with any sentiments and possibilities of guile within. I wanted to ensure that nothing else was influencing my love for her than love itself. I added another of the psalmist's prayers to my prayer list

> *"Search me, O God and know my heart. Try me and know my anxieties; And see if there is any wicked way in me. And lead me in the way everlasting."*
>
> **— (Psalm 139:23- 24)**

Our hearts have the capacity to outsmart their own bearers, and I know my heart is no exception. The prophet Jeremiah nailed it in

Jeremiah 17:9 when he said. *"The heart is deceitful above all things and beyond cure. Who can understand it?"*

The 18th Century hymn writer Robert Robinson in his famous hymn, *"Come Thou Fount of Every Blessing"* agrees with these words. He brilliantly exposes our internal struggles in this song:

"Like a fetterBind my wandering heart to thee Prone to wander, Lord I feel it.Prone to leave the God I love Here's my heart, O take and seal it Seal it for Thy court above."

I was praying often when I was considering proposing to Tracey. Being a naturally cautious person, I understood the weight of the commitment I was about to enter when I asked this most beautiful girl to marry me. As I did so, I wanted it to be from the purity of my heart devoid of any deceit.

Love that Leaves No Question

The way God chose to answer those prayers caught me off guard and completely blew me away. Just days before my planned marriage proposal, Tracey told me she had something very important she wanted to discuss with me first. At that stage, there was hardly anything about each other we didn't already know, and this included the things that were happening around us daily. So,

I was a bit concerned about what it could be that I didn't already know. I was even more concerned about the timing, just when I was getting ready to ask the most important question.

Understandably, I could hardly wait for this all-important information. Later that day, Tracey sent me an email that completely blew me away, to say the least. The content of her email was unbelievable to me. I had never met anyone who was considering what she said she wanted to do in her message. Even as a Christian, I did not know anyone who would dare to love an absolute stranger literally as Jesus would. I read her mail many times and with each reading, my personal view of what's important in life was deeply impacted.

In her email, she mentioned that as a part of their ministry to the Gypsy kids and the poor people of Albania, they had a situation where a little Albanian girl was critically ill with kidney failure, and her only hope of living was to get a kidney transplant. However, the trouble was that they could not find any willing donors. I continued reading the lengthy email, and my heart rate increased as I eventually arrived at her main point. My suspicions were true. Tracey was considering being a kidney donor for this random, poor, Albanian girl. She was willing to donate one of her kidneys to save a total stranger who had no connection whatsoever to her.

She had spoken to her parents about her decision and it was my turn to run it past me.

That was the moment of truth for me. That was the reality as far as my eyes could see. I was at the stage where I was rehearsing my words and planning the right time to propose to Tracey, but now, I had to step back, wait, and ask myself the tough question: did I still want to go ahead with the proposal when the prospect was, I could be getting married to a girl with one kidney? I did not have a good night's sleep in those couple of days that followed as I processed the various ramifications of her decision. This was indeed a serious test for the authenticity of my love for her.

As I processed this, my heart was drawn deeper and deeper unto Tracey. I knew that I could not endanger my life like that for a stranger. More than ever before, my heart and love went out to her. I knew I had made the right choice to marry her. Her love left no question in my heart of the authenticity of the love God so richly poured out in my heart for her. I knew I had found a godly girl whom I could trust my heart with. I knew I had found a loving girl worth pursuing in this journey of life.

In the quietness of my heart, I could feel God do His work as He straightened out a longstanding misconception of what is important and what it means to be successful in life. I came through that season of my life a better man and certainly a more loving person.

By that one act, Tracey opened up a fountain of God's love I didn't realize was still around. After this, I knew I had found the love of my life and my answer to my long-standing Psalm 143:8 prayer. When God was done with what He wanted to do in my heart, I discovered the beautiful thing about this story. The whole time, God had it all figured out. He was after my heart and when He was done with His intended heart surgery, it was not necessary for my wife to give her kidney to the girl. Her act of love for this Albanian girl inspired someone else from Albania to come forward and donate the kidney that saved the precious girl's life.

Reflection

> *"There is never adventure quite like being hooked up with the creator of the heavens and earth who is personally involved in our lives as our father."*
>
> **— R. Akubuiro**

May God daily draw our hearts more and more to Him, so we can continue to draw love nutrients from His inexhaustible reservoir to love Him first and then the people He brings to us as only Jesus would.

PART 2

Living On The Edge

CHAPTER FOUR

Pressing Forward In The Face Of Adversity

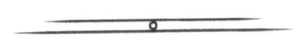

"He is no fool who gives what he cannot keep, to gain what he cannot lose."

— Jim Elliot

Dare to Dream

The desire to meaningfully contribute to the world around me and positively impact my sphere of influence has been a personal goal for a very long time. I understood the importance of higher education in reaching that goal, and I was determined against the odds, to get the best education possible. Propelled by this desire, I maximized every chance to visit the British Council library in Lagos, the national scholarship board, and the embassies of several countries in Lagos to inquire about their scholarship opportunities for Nigerians.

Following up on my research, I applied for as many of these scholarships as I was eligible for. At least, I was impressed that some of them got back to me. Curtin University in Perth, Western Australia where I now live, was one of those universities I contacted.

Sometimes dreams don't always come true, but they have the capacity to inspire others. This was exactly what happened in my case. My older brother made the effort to study overseas. He worked hard to accomplish that goal, but the odds were against him, and it became overwhelmingly difficult for him. However, some of what was left of those dreams were beneficial to me. He had some international student prospectuses from world-renowned universities. When I found these prospectuses on his bookshelf, they became my favourite handbooks. As expected, reading those foreign student prospectuses kindled my dream of one day making it to those universities as a student.

Japanese Scholarship Adventure

The defining moment of this season of my life between the end of high school and university occurred when I applied for a scholarship offered by the Japanese ministry of education, for students living in developing countries, known as Monbusho scholarship. From my research, I learned about this scholarship and realized that I had met the required criteria. I did not waste any time in starting the very long and rigorous application process. As part of the process, I had to get several medical check-ups including X-rays, vaccinations, as well as other supporting documents.

Determined to meet all the requirements and get all the supporting documents together in time for submission, I went to work on it. I had about two weeks to get the documentation ready and submitted. I was determined to give it my best shot. I was up early morning chasing those documents in the various designated places across Lagos. Sure enough, I got all the required paperwork together in time, except for a chest X-ray report.

Unfortunately, in Nigeria at the time, getting an X-ray result and feedback could take a couple of weeks. I closely followed up the X-ray results until I had less than two days to the deadline for submission. By this time, my patience was beginning to wear thin. I had to spend the entire day at the Lagos State University Teaching Hospital (LSUTH) trying to talk to any staff member at the radiology department of the hospital who would listen to me about my plight.

Eventually, I had an audience with the person in charge, and he gave me his word that the X-ray report would be ready first thing in the morning of the next day. I could sense the sad possibility that my worst nightmare could be on the horizon. However, I was still hopeful that I would have plenty of time to submit my application to the Japanese embassy in Victoria Island Lagos before the Friday 4 p.m. deadline. But this would be dependent on whether or not the person in charge would honour his words to me. Honestly, from my experience with them that entire week, it would have to take an act of God for any success at this stage.

Finally, the Friday deadline arrived. I turned up as early as I had done days before, at the LSUTH ready to pick up my X-ray report and hop on to any available taxi to the Japanese Embassy in Victoria Island, about 22 kilometres away, in very interesting traffic conditions — to be polite. I had all the other completed paperwork in a big brown envelope ready to go. I was just waiting for the X-ray report.

By this time, I was very exhausted yet hopeful that my X-ray results would be the first on the list as promised by the person in charge. Well, just around 1 p.m. after much waiting and pacing around, I finally heard my name yelled out. And there it was, the X-ray report was finally in my hand. As planned, I hopped into the next available taxi I could find and started the race against time. I needed to be at the Japanese embassy before their closing time of 4 p.m. By this time, I had less than two and a half hours to navigate through Lagos' congested peak time traffic to the other side of Lagos Island.

After about an hour of a slow movement in the traffic, I had enough and decided to take "Okada," which is a motorbike that is usually not the safest public transport option for places like Lagos. But I didn't have many options. All I wanted to do was to make it to that Japanese Embassy by some means before the 4 p.m. deadline. As the taxi pulled over for me to hop on to the motorbike, I noticed that it was starting to rain. Great! As if I needed rain to cool me down from the heat of the stress I was in at the time. The odds were clearly against me. With heightened stress levels, wet clothes, and a big brown envelope under my shirt sandwiched in-between my body and the back of the cyclist, all I could do was to look up to God from whom my help comes, and hope for the best.

At last, I made it to the Japanese Embassy at exactly 4 p.m. in one piece. I made my way quickly to the reception gate only to be informed that they had just closed. I tried to explain my plight to the security man at the gate, but he was completely uninterested in my story. I asked if I could submit my application anyway, but his answer was very short and clear: "No, we are closed!" I didn't accept that and insisted he listened to my story, but even that did not make any difference. When I realized I was not going to make any progress with him, I asked if he would be willing to take my application pack from me as I had literary placed all the necessary documentation in the brown envelope. Going back home with that envelope would add to the pain of my ordeal. Without saying a word, he took the envelope from me and shut the gate behind him. I am pretty sure he threw that envelope in the bin because I never heard from them again.

As sad and disappointing as this experience was, I went back home that day relieved. I guess because it was all over at last but also because I could sense within my heart that there's more to all that happened in that process than bad luck. Somehow, I knew that it was a typical scenario of God closing a door. But I also knew that if He closed one door, He would open another somewhere else. As the scripture says in Revelation 3:7 *"These are the words of Him who is holy and true, who holds the keys of David. What he opens no one can shut, and what he shuts no one can open."* (NIV)

Strangely, instead of grieving this missed opportunity to study in Japan, I found myself thankful for the future doors God would open. This experience opened my eyes to my limitations and helped bring me to the place when I could surrender my long-standing ambitions to pursue a scholarship overseas to God. That was the end of my struggles to study overseas. This did not happen because I had given up on that dream, but from personal experience it certainly makes sense, the words of the apostle Paul in Romans 9:16, *"It's not of him that wills, nor of him who runs, but God that shows mercy."*

After that experience, I left Lagos and went back to my little village South-east of Nigeria to take up the role of youth missionary with Scripture Union, and to take the Nigerian University entrance exam. I guess I could say that the words of Jim Elliot best describe the lesson from this experience. *"He's no fool that gives what he cannot keep, to gain what he cannot lose."*

Rural and Rugged Adventures

The decision to willingly follow God's direction back to the village was again life-changing. It was a memorable journey every step of the way. This decision was in stark contrast to my journey to Lagos because it felt as if I was sailing in the direction of the wind as opposed to sailing against it. One little door after another kept springing open before me. Maybe, it was not as grand as traveling overseas on a scholarship, but it was fulfilling and satisfying nonetheless.

During this time, I started a mentorship program for young leaders in my community. Together, we began a community Christian youth movement, which produced amazing transformation in the lives of young people in the village and the neighbouring communities. We saw evidence-based community transformation in the village and in the lives of these young people. Many who once caused trouble in the village became positive role models and valued members of the community.

A couple of them have gone on to be pastors and leaders at different levels of society.

As part of my role as a youth missionary with Scripture Union during this gap year, I was helping one of the zones (Ugiri-Mbama) to plan its annual end of the year camping event at another village called Amauzari. During this time of working with the young people, I took the university entry examination offered by the Nigerian Joint Administration and Matriculation Board (JAMB). This was an entrance examination required to study at Nigerian universities. In that examination, everyone writes down the three universities they want to enter in their order of preference. The applicant is restricted to those choices depending on the cut off mark of each school.

A couple of weeks before the camp meeting was due to start, I received a message from JAMB about my acceptance into a Bachelor of Science degree program at the Federal University of Technology Owerri (FUTO). Now, this was very interesting for a couple of reasons. First, FUTO was none of my three choices and secondly, I wanted to study biochemistry or a medical- related course and never knew that the FUTO was offering that course at the time. FUTO was also one of the most competitive in the country, and I wanted all of my choices to count.

In 1999, I was accepted to study biochemistry at one of Nigeria's elite universities: Federal University of Technology Owerri (FUTO). This was a rallying point for some of the finest young minds across the country. The thought of studying at one of Nigeria's elite universities was certainly exciting for me and an awesome open door.

Life-Shaping Word

One of the beautiful things about being a part of God's family is that you hear the Father's voice in your heart. Weeks before setting out for university, I wanted a word from God that would give me some sense of direction, as I stepped out into the future as a student and beyond. And during one of the meetings with the young people at the Scripture Union camp, God sent me the scripture in Proverbs Chapter 24:27 through a random participant in the camp during prayer time. Somehow, I knew that was what I was waiting for.

> "Prepare your outside work, make it fit for yourself in the field;
> and afterward build your house."
> **— (Proverbs 24:27)**

There it was, just a random Bible verse, but as it turned out, that verse had indeed become the road map that has defined the paths I have taken these past twenty years of my life. This scripture has provided a sense of direction in times of confusion and when I had to make multiple choices about my next step. It has ensured clarity and informed my priorities at every stage of my life for these many years. Who said God's sure Word is not worth waiting for?

As I walked into FUTO, I knew I had just taken the first step in that journey of preparing my outside work. I also knew I needed to look to God for clarity for the many other steps ahead of me. As expected, the way forward had many sharp turns along the way, and I had to lean hard on His grace. It was a work-in-progress scenario but God was leading me. Little did I know that I was on a six-year crash course journey of transformation that would leave a life-long impact on the life of this obscure village boy.

Reflection

> *"God made you as you are in order to use you as He planned."*
> ### — S.C. McAuley

> *"May the sum of our life experiences and challenges become a tool in God's hands for His noble purpose in your generation."*
> ### — R. Akubuiro

CHAPTER FIVE

Seasons of Unseen Struggles

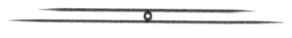

"Fight the good fight of faith."

— (1 Timothy 6:12)

The Power of Influence

I always remember my little village of Umudim with fondness and a sense of concern. I had the privilege of following several cultural metamorphoses that have taken place in that little community over the two-and- a-half decades I lived there. Within that period, I have seen the transformations and the deteriorations around social and cultural value systems. Umudim has a state-run secondary school named the Umudim Secondary School. This was built to be one of the best secondary schools in the state with boarding facilities.

Unfortunately, the then state-of-the-art teachers' quarters and dormitories, as well as other essential infrastructures are all dilapidated and in ruins. The collapse of the village school's infrastructure was followed by the dwindling of the interest of young people in education. As a consequence, an increasing number of young people were seduced to quicker but dishonest ways of making money.

In the middle of this dark season, I found myself in this community. I was in class with students who hardly wanted to do anything in school. This is a stark contradiction of the cultural values of my tribe's people of Ibo. Igbo people are very hardworking and believe strongly in education as the key to freedom from the cycle of poverty. There was a common understanding that a sure way to break the generational cycle of poverty is education. This understanding encouraged parents to make sacrifices to raise money, so they can send their children to school. The Umudim as a community can boast of producing several prominent and influential people in the wider Nigerian society. Many of these people have distinguished themselves in their fields of endeavours.

For many years, these eminent individuals in our community became mentors and role models for my generation. Their commitment to excellence and success in their careers were a source of inspiration for many of us. They provided much-needed influence and encouragement to the younger generation, and I was one of the recipients of their encouraging gestures. At some point, a group of these professionals came together to form "The Old Boys Association." This group gave out cash prizes and scholarships to the best students in different subjects from the local community. I was privileged to receive some of those prices on several occasions. Yet, as influential as these guys were in the lives of the younger generation, their impact did not match what was about to come.

The mid- 1990s and the 2000s officially welcomed what became a season of internet fraud commonly known as 419 in Nigeria. My village soon became the epicentre of that movement. It was not long before we started seeing young people drop out of school and join some internet fraud mogul in Lagos. After a year or two, they would return to the village with the latest sports cars and building classy homes. Unfortunately, the entire incentive for hard work and education was out the window. As you would imagine, this get-rich-quick syndrome won over the hearts of the majority of young people I grew up with. You had to be strong not to be swayed by the seductive influence of the evil spiritual forces behind that movement.

I sincerely cannot take credit for the strength to withstand the enormous seductive influence of that season. It was my faith in God that gave me the courage to stand firm during this terrifying time. In retrospect, I realized how much of God's sustaining grace kept my feet from those alluring slippery slopes. In many ways, it felt like Daniel and his friends who chose not to bow to the image of the king of Babylon, or eat the food from the king's table as was recorded in Daniel 1:8. *"But Daniel purposed in his heart that he would not defile himself with the portion of the king's delicacies, nor with the wine which he drank."*

Line in the Sand Moment

One cool evening as I was coming back from a friend's house along the main street of the village, I stopped to say hi to some of the young people at one of the village's popular hangout joints. One of the guys by the name of Chigozie wanted to talk to me about what was on his mind. In the course of our conversation, he raised the subject of 419- internet fraud and how he believed it was a new way to break free from poverty. He felt it would help develop our community. At that moment, I still remember a strong sense of God's presence that I felt as we talked. I dared to share the spiritual truth about the evil influence of 419 to the community and future generations who participated in those criminal activities. I warned that they would have to pay for the wicked acts they committed against innocent people around the world. 419 may seem to be a glamorous act at present for these young perpetrators, but sooner or later, the untold pains and anguish they have caused their innocent victims will come after them, just exactly as the bible stated it in Numbers 32:23 (KJV). *"Be sure your sin will find you out."*

He listened with interest as I attempted to answer some of his many questions. With every word I spoke, I felt inner courage to talk even more, and he listened attentively. I shared with him about God's plans to give us life in abundance. I talked about His plans to prosper people in genuine businesses and professions as we work diligently in pursuit of His purpose for our lives.

After a while, He abruptly interrupted me with this confronting question: "Tell me the names of people in this village who are examples of this God's prosperity you are talking about." An awkward silence followed. You could hear a pin drop. I completely understood his question, and since I was in an answering mode, I was literally scanning through the length and breadth of the village in my mind in search of an example of a godly prosperous man to prove my point. This was no time for a sermon on the mountain. He was asking for facts and figures, and we both knew it. Everybody knew everybody in the community and could tell you the stories of how everyone makes money.

As my mind raced through the village, kindred by kindred a few names popped up for consideration. I finally presented a couple of names. Prominent among them was a successful civil engineer who contributed positively to the community and another one who was a much- respected successful businessman. Unfortunately, both of these people had only recently come to faith in Christ. Before I even finished mentioning their names, Chigozie had already double-crossed me by alleging that these men had already made their money in dodgy deals before they became Christians.

In the heat of that moment, I felt a sense of God's presence and just as I was about to concede defeat, what felt like bubbles of courage fired up inside me. I had an answer for him, but I couldn't place my finger on what it was exactly. Suddenly, an almost audible yet still, small voice of the Holy Spirit whispered, "So what are you?" I didn't understand the point of that still small voice at first, but it soon made sense. God was asking me to mention my name to him. But that was a bit too much and somewhat a ridiculous joke. At least, that's what I thought.

At that split moment, I dared to think of myself as God's answer to Chigozie's question, even though that sounded worse than conceding defeat. Strengthened with unusual courage, I looked Chigozie in the eye and confidently spoke up. "I may not be able to name anyone that will satisfy you right now, but you're looking at one." I was expecting a laugh or an expression of disgust, but I was so surprised by this response. He said "OK." He was happy with that. Knowing the kind of person Chigozie is, I am still very curious to know what exactly he saw in me in that moment, that made him agree with my answer to his question. I walked away from the encounter knowing that the line was drawn in the sand, and my work was cut out for me. This experience refreshed my understanding of God's purpose for my life concerning the lives of the young people in that local community. Another lesson I walked away with from that encounter is that what happens in our lives is not just about us. There are generations out there who are waiting to be inspired by our stories of courage, love, and faith. There is a generation waiting for us to wake up from the bed of ordinary life and live for so much more. I completely understood that I had just raised the bar for myself by making those courageous declarations. However, I have come to anchor my hope in the words of Philippians 2:13 *"For it is God who works in you to will and to act in order to fulfil his good purpose."* I was just beginning to understand that it has never been about me the whole time, but about God and what He is able to do even with the least of us for His glory.

The Reality of the Fight

It was not long before we started a Christian youth movement in the village. God poured out His Spirit on the young people, turned their hearts away from 419, and focused them on Him. People were beginning to see the menace of 419. They recognized it as the evil it really is. Thankfully, the emphasis on education as a path for sustainable development was reinstated.

A couple of months later, I had the most unforgettable experience that opened my eyes to the reality of the spiritual warfare I was engaged in right there in my village. We had just finished a weekend outreach program with the young people at the Umuduruonyoma Christian Youths' Movement. I was living at the university then. I came back from school for the weekend youth event in the village and had to go back to school early on Monday morning. As I was getting ready that morning, I heard this strange concern to pray against the revival of the evil influence of the 419 in my village. After spending time praying, I went to the bus stop just across the road from my house to catch a bus to Owerri.

As I waited for the bus to turn up, someone pulled over right in front of me in a very classy sports car. There he was, one of my school mates who had made a lot of money from 419. It would have been disrespectful to reject his offer of a lift, especially as he was heading in my direction. So, I hopped in, and we chatted along the way. Again, I could sense something in my spirit, but I was still not sure what it was until I got to my destination. I thanked him for the lift and just as I opened the door to get out, he opened his glove box and handed me a bundle of cash. I was put on the spot right there. There was no question about what I should do, but I was in a very difficult financial situation in school at that stage, with several university fees that were overdue. That money would have certainly come in handy. He and I knew it was a trap I would walk away from or fall into. Again, God's grace was enough for me to do the right thing. I voiced my gratitude for the thought and lift but most politely declined to receive the money from him. As he drove off, I could almost hear the angels rejoicing. I was very encouraged and strengthened to keep fighting the good fight.

Treading on Dangerous Ground

During my third year at the university, I had the privilege of serving as the coordinator of all the Christian fellowships on campus. This position allowed me to participate in shaping the value system of the university and setting the spiritual atmosphere of that community. One of the challenges that had long confronted the university authorities across the country was the students' involvement in the occult. Student cultism has secretly gained ground in Nigerian universities, and every year, there are reports of killings, rituals and other diabolic activities. By this time, FUTO had become a notorious hide-out for some of the most dangerous student cult groups, and this was becoming a big problem for the university authorities. The Christian fellowships on campus were at the forefront of addressing this growing social problem.

After many prayer and outreach campaigns, we decided to courageously stand up as the body of Christ on the campus against cultism. We were ready to push back the encroaching spiritual darkness of cultism on our campus. We started praying for directions and soon came up with a plan for a campus community-wide anti-cult weekend campaign. Initially, this sounded like a crazy idea. It was going to be a dangerous undertaking, but we were ready for it, or at least I thought I was ready for it. The university authorities were very happy to see that we were courageous enough to take on these giants, and they gave us all the support we needed.

Soon the anti-cult campaign was the big news, not only in the FUTO campus but in the entire state and the other neighbouring universities as well. As the countdown to the event began, the reality of the magnitude of this spiritual confrontation was starting to unfold. Feedback from the cult groups was received and threats to my life and the lives of my team members were made. This was no child's play. Everybody knew how cruel these cult groups are and the evil they are capable of. We knew that their threats were not empty words, but somehow, God clothed us with courage and boldness as we planned, until one particular night.

The Battle in the Garden

About half a kilometre walk from the hostels is a garden formally known as "The Love Garden," but has been renamed to "The Prayer Garden." This has become one of my favourite places in all the university. I have spent time pouring out my heart to God in prayer beside the concrete benches there. It had become a safe place to hide out for me and many others. You can hardly walk into the prayer garden without hearing the voice of someone, somewhere around the corner reaching out to God in prayer. But this night was a bit different. There was an unusual stillness and darkness that sent out an unwelcoming sensation. This is my turf, my safe place, and I was not going to give in to any unwelcoming thoughts and feelings. I was there for business with heaven.

As I made my way through the bushy walkway and the overgrown grass to get to my usual spot in the garden, I sensed a strange feeling of darkness around me. By this time, I was worried about the strangeness of the dark feeling that surrounded this usually peaceful place. I could breathe in fear with every breath. And every step I took felt heavier than the one before. I tried to brave the feeling and push forward until I was completely frozen with fear. My hair was on edge, and my heart was pounding. I was surrounded by thick darkness. I couldn't see a metre in front of me. It was a very strange feeling. I felt an oppressive presence in the darkness as if someone cruel was right there waiting for me behind the darkness. As I weighed my options and considered my next line of action —which was to run as fast as I could before whoever was in that darkness showed up. A sense of strength and courage rose up within me. I started praying in the spirit as loudly as I possibly could. And as I prayed, more doses of strength came through. I had a choice to make. At that moment, I came to the reality of what it means to truly count the cost for following Jesus. This was a sort of litmus test to determine how much I was willing to put on the line to follow Jesus.

Involuntarily, I found myself questioning if the entire anti-cult campaign was worth my life. Do I really believe in God that much? How would I respond if that evil being in the covers of darkness turned out to be one of the executioners of a cult group? What if he had a gun to my face and fingers on the trigger demanding that I denounce Jesus and pull out of the campaign or get my head blown off? These questions resounded in my mind.

This was a very tough place to be. As I stood there frozen with fear, my natural response was to run away from that place as fast as I possibly could, or stand firm in courage and face the fear. The choice I make would determine victory or defeat, but could also mean life or death. Again, the line was clearly drawn in the sand and there was no middle ground. I could imagine the executioner demanding that I deny Jesus and call off the anti-cult campaign or die. Fear made what was going on in my mind very real. In that moment, I thought of the authenticity of my experiences with Jesus since the moment He found me in that little classroom in the village. There was no question about the sincerity of my decision many years ago to follow Jesus. Turning back now or backing down was not an option. He is all I had always wanted to live for. I was ready right there to stand my ground and confront that spirit of fear.

I decided one of two things would have to happen. Worst case scenario, I would have my head blown off if that executioner pulled that trigger, but before my back hit the ground, I would wake up in glory at the feet of Jesus with the angels welcoming me home. That would not be a bad way to go home, I thought. Another possible thing that could happen is if God chose to stop that gun from going off, that would be a next-level victory story. When this was settled in my heart, that thick cloud of darkness was immediately lifted, and that victory was sealed. I had the most amazing hours of prayer in the garden that night, and we had the most amazing anti-cult campaign a couple of days later, with many cult members coming openly to denounce their membership in cult groups and to turn their lives to Christ. Some of them grew in their walk with God to become leaders in the various campus fellowships.

Reflection

> "What happens in our lives is not just about us. There are generations out there who are waiting to be inspired by our stories of courage, acts of love, and expressions of faith. They are waiting for us to wake up from the bed of ordinary life and live for so much more."
>
> **— R. Akubuiro**

CHAPTER SIX

Seasons of Stretching and Straightening

"Oftentimes the best foot forward is a swift kick in the seat of the pants."

— Hugh Myrrh

A Journey out of My Comfort Zone

A journey out of my comfort zone would be a better way to describe my experiences going through myuniversity studies at the Federal University of Technology Owerri (FUTO). I came into FUTO with a sound spiritual foundation as the only thing I had going for me. Every other aspect of my world view was shaped by all I knew from the village. I was ignorant of what life looked like in an average middle-class Nigerian family. I remember watching Nigerian movies at friends' houses with the sole goal of having an insight into what the middle and upper-class families looked like. I had some embarrassing moments as

I adjusted to life with my mates in school. It was interesting how naive and uninformed I was about a lot of things.

On one occasion, a friend had an asthma attack in school, and someone had to rush to get his inhaler from the hostel. I offered to go but thankfully, someone else went ahead of me. The trouble was I knew absolutely nothing about asthma and inhalers. The only inhaler I knew about was the Vicks inhaler. So, you could imagine how grateful I was to God that I was not the one who eventually ran that errand. When I listened to the conversations of my peers about places they had been and their life experiences, I wondered which planet I was coming from. I got even more intimidated when I compared my village experiences with theirs. At first, I didn't think I had anything to contribute to the sophisticated people I was with.

Before this time, I had compared myself to kids in the village who were worse off than me, and I had sort of become a village champion. Understandably, I didn't expect an easy road going to one of the top universities in Nigeria, which is the rallying point for the best students in terms of background and academic achievements. To a great extent, I clearly understood my limitations as a poor village boy, and I planned on being intentional about respecting that status and not get in anyone's way.

Growing up after my father passed away, Mum always admonished us to always remember our poor estate. Even though my immediate family was poor, we have always had very rich relatives. Living so close to wealth yet so far from it, I learned to manage the dynamics of that coexistence. I was sort of content with our side of that divide and had made my peace with that, but I was hopeful that God would help me break that cycle as it's not a particularly pleasant place to be.

A strikingly unpleasant memory for me in the village happened when a wealthy relative of ours visited our home during the Christmas season. It was on a Sunday evening after church. I was playing with the other kids when the white Mercedes Benz car pulled into our compound. We were very excited and all over the car. I still remember what one of the older boys around the car said to me when I touched the Mercedes Benz logo in the front of the car bonnet. He rebuked me for touching the logo and with a disdainful look, he told me I was not worth the cost of that Mercedes logo in the market. I was not sure if he intended it to be a joke or not, but I walked away from that car determined not to be a loser in life. It becomes natural to adapt to such environment and build up defences to protect your poor self in your comfort zone when you are growing up in a place like that.

Unfortunately for me, the Federal University of Technology Owerri was nothing like my village. From the onset, I consciously established four ground rules for myself. The first one was to stay out of any kind of trouble and concentrate on my studies. The second rule was not to become a member of any association or group. The third one was to mind my own business and never get into anything that will expose my naivety and poor background.

And finally, to serve God in some quiet capacity and make my contribution to His kingdom in FUTO anonymously.

I did well in staying within the confines of these ground rules for about a week, just in time to attend a student prayer conference organized by Students Christian Movement (SCM), a group I had served with during my secondary school years. I attended that conference on my own as I normally do, but made the mistake of writing FUTO in the school column in the attendance register. On the last day of the conference, one of the participants who happened to come from FUTO curiously asked for my name. Everything changed when I told him.

Apparently, all the delegates from FUTO were asking around and very eager to meet this Richard. I was not very impressed by their excitement to meet me as I was quite happy with my anonymous status. By the time we got back to the campus, they sought me out and invited me to the Student Christian Movement Campus Fellowship (SCM), one of the largest campus fellowships on that campus, with over two hundred active student members.

The First Surprise

As I looked around in the large hall filled with students, I felt somewhat intimidated and was certainly happy I had adopted those set of ground rules. My comfortable little space was not ready in a hundred years for the surprise that was around the corner. During the announcements, the president went up front to share the highlights of the prayer conference. Toward the end of his speech, he added that they had prayerfully identified the year coordinator for the first-year students. Now, my heart started to beat a bit faster hoping against hope that whatever he did, my name would never by any chance, slip out of his mouth. To cut a long story short, he called my name as the freshmen student coordinator. With this, everybody applauded before even seeing who this Richard was. At that moment, I did not know what to think. I froze for a split second and tried to assure myself that this was not happening. Before I realized what was going on, people gathered around me to give me a hand to stand up, and the rest was history.

In this role, a couple of things were very apparent to me. First, I knew I didn't have what it would take to lead those brilliant students, and I also knew that with God, nothing is impossible. So, my plan of action was to lean hard on God for even something as simple as introducing myself to the group. I will always remember my first meeting with this amazing team of brilliant young minds. I was so intimidated by their command of the English language and their backgrounds. In our first meeting, as we went around the circle introducing ourselves, the secondary schools we attended and said any other things we wanted about ourselves. It became clearer how much of God I needed if I was going to be of any good to them as their leader, considering my level of exposure in comparison to theirs.

The interesting thing here was that God truly became my source of strength during this season. I quickly learned to wait on the Lord, leaning in hard and trusting His grace for even the simplest component of my role as a leader. The sense of God's presence soon became my source of strength as I struggled with my low self-esteem. This group of freshmen known as "Mighty Generation" grew to become amazing leaders, who served in various capacities in leadership positions in FUTO and continued to excel in their careers around the world today.

The Second Surprise

The first year ended in peace, as my confidence grew and I slowly got a handle on the leadership of the Mighty Generation. I was hoping for a smoother second year without drama and any other surprises, but you can't be so sure. It was time for the SCM executive election, and the electoral committee was formed. Not long after, I was invited by the committee to possibly consider taking an executive position in the fellowship. I made it clear that I was not ready for leadership at that level and thought they had heard me, but they must have believed I was being humble about my inexperience and naivety. When it comes to leading people as mature and experienced as the ones I met in the SCM in any capacity, I knew that I was not ready. I would have been happy to have them as my lecturers and mentors, so leading them at any capacity was completely out of range for me. I was very clear about this in my meeting with the electoral committee, or so I thought.

On the election night, I was not concerned because I was convinced that I had nothing to worry about. Unfortunately, I was wrong again. After walking through all the different executive offices, the last position was that of the executive president. The responsibilities were readout, and to my dismay, my name was called along with one other person as the nominated candidates for the position. Once again, I was in the same place dealing with the insecurities and was wondering why God was taking me on this path. By the end of that evening, I was elected the executive president of SCM FUTO. What in the world does a village boy know about being a president of a campus fellowship in one of Nigeria's prestigious universities? Many other thoughts similar to that raced through my mind.

I certainly had a lot of work to do to live up to the high standard my predecessor had set. Emeka- the out-going president was one of the most dynamic young leaders I had ever met. There was no way I was going to fit into his shoes. I needed God to take me through a season of intensive leadership development. The challenge of the moment felt like a giant before me, and I did not immediately see the relevance of the leadership skills I acquired as a leader in the village until later in my role.

Through this leadership season, I learned to depend completely on God and find my strength and confidence in His presence and promises. Special moments of encouragement for me during this challenging time of leadership came from one of the respectable members of the fellowship — Sorochi. During this period, there was usually water scarcity in the hostels, and sometimes the university authorities had to arrange water trucks to deliver water to students. Sorochi shared a dream he had about me. He dreamed of a fountain springing up from my room at the SCM secretariat and flooding the entire school. It brought so much joy and relief to students across the campus and spread into the other campuses and beyond. I was so encouraged to hear a prophetic word about my place in God's agenda for that campus. This revelation brought a renewed vigour in my journey and challenged me to give my utmost to His Highest. That one year of service as the president of SCM FUTO became one of the most intensive seasons of learning and growth in my life as a person and a leader.

The Third Surprise

When you consider where I was coming from and my initial decision to remain anonymous and not to get formally engaged with campus fellowship, you can appreciate how far away from my comfort zone I was. Even with this exposure to leadership, there was so much of me that still naturally gravitated to my comfort zone.

After my first two consecutive years of service in student leadership, I soon realized that God was getting me ready for a greater challenge on that campus and beyond. Then came my third year in School, after serving my Fellowship — SCM as the president, I was nominated to represent my fellowship at the Joint Christian Campus body — Joint Christian Campus Fellowship (JCCF). And there, I was elected to be the president of the Joint Christian Campus Fellowship. It was a very influential position representing about two-thirds of the entire university student population. This was not the journey I imagined, but I was grateful to God that He took me through that experience even though it was stretching. The lessons were worth it.

Reflection

"Those who walk with Christ by faith know the meaning of wonder in their daily lives. His wonders are seen in so-called little things, such as a flower, or bird, or a baby's smile. And they're seen in big things as well, such as the courage to say 'No', or the strength to keep going when the road is difficult. Little things become big when they're touched by the wonder of Christ."

— Warren W. Wiersbe

PART 3

Living Hope

CHAPTER SEVEN

Life More Abundantly

"I come that they may have life and life more abundantly."

— (John 10:10)

Rural, Raw and Rugged

During one of our rural outreach events, I met Chikaku. He happened to come from my village. Chikaku was a young man who had been in trouble with the law a few times. He had dropped out of the local community school for a number of reasons, which included the complexity of his family dynamics and his dislike for authority. Chikaku was one of those kids you would not want hanging around your house or going out with your kids. To prove himself, he got involved in

petty crimes and other anti-social behaviours. Anyone who cared to look would see that this precious young life was headed for a precipice. It would be just a matter of time before he got himself into major trouble.

The memory of my meeting with Chikaku that afternoon and the events that transpired afterward is a simple representation of how God cares for the "least of these." It has become like a glance through the eyes of God. It not only reminded me of God's love for the poor and the vulnerable people among us, but also His care for me in my low estate. I sort of could imagine how Nathaniel felt when Jesus told him in the gospel of John 1:48, *"I saw you while you were still under the fig tree before Philip called you."* At this stage in this disciple's life, he was completely unaware of the depth of God's work in his life, but heaven was waiting for this moment to catch his attention. God cares about each of our stories. He certainly did get Chikaku's attention.

I heard someone yell out my name as I walked past an AOG church building in Umudim. I turned my eyes to see who it could be. Chikaku, was the last person in a hundred years I could imagine walking out of a church building. Unless of course he was there to cause trouble. But why a church building and what did he want with me? These questions raced through my mind as my eyes caught the sight of him, before I even spoke a word. To be completely honest, all I wanted to do was run off and pretend I didn't hear him, but I was glad I did the right thing. Something was certainly different about him that day. There was a great deal if softness and grace in his voice, as he walked closer to me. I also saw a visible gracefulness that would not normally be associated with the Chikaku everybody in the village knew.

I didn't know what to think. Just before I gathered my thoughts to ask him how I could help, he said, "Bro Chidi, I have been looking for you." If it was just those words that I heard without seeing his face as he said them, I would have been seriously worried, but his facial expression was an assurance that something divine was going on within the heart of this lonely young man. As I looked at him, I saw a

lovely, vulnerable, and needy young man crying out for help. It was as if God had granted me a momentary glimpse through His eyes to see the same Chikaku but in the light of God's love. The songwriter Geron Davis couldn't have put it better when he said:

"The justice of God saw what I had done, but mercy saw me through the Son, not what I was, but what I could be, that's how mercy saw me."

For about two hours, Chikaku unpacked his story as I listened intently. I was humbled to hear the depth of God's love and the length He is willing to go in pursuit of us. God had used a series of events in Chikaku's life to get his attention. Most recently, it was a simple dream that reminded him of God's love for him personally. When he woke up from his sleep, my name came to him and that was when he started looking for me. It was humbling and somewhat reassuring that God would trust me to be an extension of His hands to bring His love to this precious young man.

That meeting marked the start of a new beginning for Chikaku. In the months and years that followed, I saw God transform my friend into a loving godly man. He found his place in God's family and the strength to overcome a lifetime of hurt and trauma, to become a responsible member of the community. He became an inspiration and a beacon of hope to many others like him in that community.

One of the things God did in my heart from this encounter was to bring home to my heart His love for the "least of these." I felt a deep sense that God was calling me to be committed to taking the good news of His love and care to the poor and vulnerable members of our societies, but trusted Him for the details of what form and shape that would look like. This encounter was one of the inspirations that reinforced the vision of the Gospel Foundation International legacy project, an opportunity to extend God's love and good news to the poor and vulnerable members of our community.

> *"When the poor and needy are dying of thirst and cannot find water, I, the Lord God of Israel, will come to their rescue. I won't forget them."*
>
> **— (Isaiah 41:19 CEV)**

In every culture and country, irrespective of the economic status, we will always meet the likes of Chikaku at the corner of the dusty road waiting and hoping for those glimpse-through- the-eyes-of-God moments.

In 2016, I joined the OM mission ship for a two- year missionary adventure to 13 different countries across the Asian-Pacific region. In every country we visited, there were many opportunities to meet the poor and the vulnerable members of the communities, which testifies of the relentless pursuit of a loving God. This is not to say that God is not pursuing the elite and affluent members of our communities, but the focus of this book is His pursuit of the "least of these."

I have shared some of my experiences in a number of countries here below.

Alive and Free in the Philippines

One of the sad but heart-warming moments of my mission trip with the OM ship- the Doulos, was an experience in a drug rehabilitation centre in the Philippines. Our audiences were children and young people of different ages whose lives and hopes for a better future were hijacked by the tyranny of substance abuse. The heart- warming moment came when one of the young people who use to be one of them, who was a former drug addict shared about his journey to freedom and recovery in Christ. It was such a solemn moment that we could almost see hope rise in the hearts of those precious brothers and sisters as we looked into their eyes, witnessed their responses, and listened to their stories. Again, we felt the unseen hand of God's love reaching out to the "least of these."

Dark Cloud Lifted in New Zealand

Tony is a Kiwi middle-aged man who had endured hurt and heartbreaks that made him very angry with God. While waiting for a connecting train to his destination in New Zealand, he heard about the Doulos ship and decided that visiting it would be a more productive way to spend his time while he waited for his connecting train hours later. I met Tony browsing through the books on the book exhibition deck of the Doulos and started a conversation with him. He was very open and willing to share a bit about his journey and the hurt he went through. He had just experienced a painful divorce, lost the custody of his children and in his words, "lost everything." I remember sharing a bit of my story and praying with him. Then I introduced a book by Tim LaHaye – Where Is God When It Hurts – to him. We exchanged email addresses at that meeting.

A couple of months afterward, I received an email from Tony with an amazing story of transformation that happened in his life over that period. According to Tony, his hurt and depression had driven him to contemplate suicide several times, but for some reason he could only describe it as "God's mercy", that dark cloud of depression was lifted from him. In his words he said "Christ has set me free", and all he wanted to do was to help other hurting people around him experience the same freedom. He wanted to be an extension of God's hands to see the dark cloud of depression lifted off them as well. He informed me that he is now actively involved in a community program reaching out to the hurting and needy people just like he once was.

Hope in Papua New Guinea

I was invited to do a presentation at a program organized by World Vision for people living with HIV/AIDS in Papua New Guinea, what I saw opened my eyes to the living essence of this hope, especially for people facing terminal illness. Even though HIV/AIDS is no longer regarded as terminal with the advancement in the development of anti-retroviral drugs, but for many people in developing countries, it's still very much a life-threatening illness.

Many of the people living with HIV/AIDS that attended the meeting had little access to much- needed medication and nutritional support to help them maintain healthy lifestyles. However, I noticed that something was different about them from the other groups I had spoken to previously. Later, I realized what accounted for that difference was the hope they have in Christ. Many of these people in their distress and sickness had reached out to God for help and hope. This hope has become an anchor for their souls even beyond the grave. For some of them, the fear of death had lost its grip. For me, it was somewhat a sad moment, but I had not just learned a lesson about hope, but I saw hope alive.

Little Be It or Much

One of the most beautiful expressions of love from the "least of these" came to me in the remotest part of Northern Nigeria where I went for a mission exposure trip. We visited a special Islamic tribal group who are mainly nomadic and extremely poor. As part of my volunteer program, I was sent to spend two weeks with missionaries living and serving among these precious people.

The children in this culture know nothing about Western education. For many of them, the only exposure to Western education or the outside contact they will ever get is these missionaries. My host missionary introduced me to little Ibrahim. He was about 7 years of age and had become a regular visitor to the missionary base. Little Ibrahim had grown to love the missionaries and desired to help them in any little way he could. An opportunity came one day while the missionaries were playing with the kids. Something came up about buying a particular item. One of the missionary couples mentioned buying the item but that they didn't have money and couldn't get it unless God provided the money for them.

Surprisingly, little Ibrahim spoke up in his local language saying, "I don't have money but if I ever have 20 Naira, I will give it to you." They all enjoyed the moment and moved on, but for little Ibrahim, he had given his word and made a commitment. Many weeks later, Ibrahim had managed to save up 5 Naira and he walked up to the missionary to fulfil his commitment.

The gesture of little Ibrahim reminds me of the words of John Bunyan's Hymn:

"I am content with what I have, little be it or much; The Lord's contentment still I crave…"

Reflection

"Wherever you are, be there. Live life to the hilt every situation you believe to be the will of God."

— Jim Elliot

"What we are is God's gift to us. What we become is our gift to God."

— Louis Nizer

"The King will reply, 'Truly I tell you, whatever you did for one of the least of these brothers and sisters of mine, you did for me.'"

— Matthew 25:11 (NIV)

CHAPTER EIGHT

A Compelling Vision

"Ideas not coupled with action never get bigger than the brain cells they occupy."

— **George Bernard Shaw**

Where Do You Fit?

My various leadership experiences as a student, had provided amazing opportunities for personal development in every aspect of my life. There is no doubt that I graduated from FUTO with more than a bachelor's degree in biochemistry. Nevertheless, I didn't get a lot of opportunities to reach out to the poor and vulnerable people groups in the rural areas that I had a natural passion for. Unconsciously, I saw myself looking forward to the holidays to be part of outreach teams reaching out to the rural communities within my state. I did this with Scripture Union Owerri Area during my first year's long holiday of 1999/2000.

During this time, I was sent as a youth missionary to support the Scripture Union Ministry in the very rural region of Egbema zone. This was an exciting time for me, even though no one else around me saw any excitement in going to an obscure rural community to hang out with poor villagers. Serving alongside these people, I saw God at work in a dimension that is real and simple, but yet profound.

Finding My Place

Back to school after the Egbema adventure, I was looking forward to another short-term mission during the next long holiday. This time, I was hoping and planning for a more challenging experience. Something that could perhaps stretch my capacity to completely depend on the Lord. Beyond searching for adventure, I was seriously looking for "my place in the field". I wanted to understand how these interests in reaching the vulnerable and the unreached people groups could engage the lessons I was learning in school, and translate to a possible long-term initiative of some sort.

I had all these creative ideas and thought of the possibilities of using my talents, career, and hobbies on these mission adventures to make a greater impact on the lives of these needy people, but I needed help with substantiating these ideas. I figured that the one place to look for ideas would be at the office of a local missionary agency called Calvary Ministries (CAPRO). One afternoon in June 2011, I visited CAPRO's office in Owerri to inquire about their short-term mission program called Operation Joshua, and to see if they had any helpful resources.

As I sat down in the reception lounge facing a bookshelf, my eyes went straight to a particular book sitting among over a hundred others. I couldn't get my eyes off that book and finally, I stood up and picked it up. The book was Operation World by Patrick Johnstone, the 21st Century edition. I opened the first page and right in front of me were pictures of people doing a variety of creative activities in different pieces of puzzles, all fitting perfectly into the big picture. This picture captured my attention. As I tried to make sense of what the picture could represent, I read the question in bold letters on top of the picture that said: "Where do you fit?" Now, this had my full attention. I was captivated. It was certainly getting more interesting. I sat up and began to explore what the writer was talking about.

Soon I discovered he was advertising the short-term exposure program (STEP) of the Operation Mobilization outreach ship- MV Doulos. Just when I thought I had finally figured it out, things were getting even more interesting and exciting, to say the least. This was more than a coincident. The question- "Where do you fit", seemed to be directed to me. It was as personal as it can get. I knew it was exactly what I was looking for. I knew God was in this. I felt a sense of His presence at that moment, which made me want to pursue this even though it was an almost impossible undertaking, considering my economic status at that stage of my life. As I read about the STEP program and how it works, faith rose up inside of me and all I could see was God opening doors for me to participate in this program. So, I collected all the relevant information about the STEP program that I could find in the book and on their website and commenced my research about the program immediately.

Not long after, I found their email address and sent them a message expressing my interest in participating in the STEP program. And sure enough, I got a reply informing me of their planned visit to West Africa from November 2001 to January 2002. That fitted perfectly into my long holiday period. I could see God's hand behind the scene as He orchestrated each step to make it possible. However, I knew it was going to be a long shot.

As the correspondence continued and the details of the STEP program were revealed, I was informed that the date for the next

STEP program would be from mid-November 2001 to Mid-January 2002, and the countries would be Ghana and then to Togo. At that stage in my life, the prospect of going anywhere outside Nigeria was a distant dream, but I had to grow up and stand up to this prospect. I had to prepare myself for this if I was serious about embarking on this level of mission adventure.

Some of the milestones in my preparation process included getting an international passport and the required vaccinations. I had to trust God for His financial provision to get these requirements together. And sure enough, He provided the finances through the least expected people. For the first time in my life, I had that green Nigerian passport in my hands with my name and photo on it. This was one of the initial signs that it was not a distant dream anymore. It was a needed boost that strengthened my resolve to push through the other challenges that stood in the way of achieving this objective.

After a couple of weeks, I received an email from the STEP team expressing satisfaction with my application and supporting documents. But they informed me that I would be required to travel to Ghana for an interview, after which they would decide on my acceptance into the program. I soon realized it was going to be more expensive than I initially thought as I would have to travel to Ghana twice within 3 months. Unfortunately, there was no second option. There are usually no short cuts to destiny as you and I already know. Well, I accepted the invitation to the interview in Ghana and the date was scheduled.

I started another round of fundraising for this journey and thankfully, I was ready. I made it safely to Tema in Ghana, where the MV Doulos Ship was at the time. For the first time in my life, I was in a country other than Nigeria.

The journey to Ghana through four different countries' land borders was not an experience anyone would look forward to. For instance, going through the immigration checkpoint at the Seme border (Nigerian-Benin Republic border), some uniformed officials demanded to search my belongings and openly pressed me for bribes. I got into trouble with them when I insisted on not offering them bribes. The sad thing was it was done in the open, and the officials on both sides of the border were completely fine with it. Well, they finally let me go when they realized I didn't have much money anyway.

Dreams Come True

Finally, I made it to Tema, and there it was in real life, the big and white MV Doulos ship. It looked exactly as I saw in the picture, but just a bit bigger than I imagined. Seeing this magnificent ship that I had looked at a hundred times on the internet, in real life was a surreal feeling. I physically stood in awe of God for making it possible thus far. It was more than a milestone in my pursuit of the mission adventure, but a strategic step in the journey of identifying my purpose and fulfilling it.

Suddenly, there was substance to the whole idea, thoughts, and plans. It was standing right there in front of me. Wow! If you dare to see it with the eyes of faith, it's possible to see it in real life, I thought to myself. I learned so much and felt so good about the journey at that point that even if the outcome of the interview didn't go in my favour, it was OK. As it is, I have learned vital

lessons about dreams and passion in the pursuit of finding your place in this world. I was encouraged to think and dream even more, and to believe God for what may seem impossible with man as there is no impossibility with Him.

William Carey couldn't have put it better in his famous saying: *"Expect great things from God; attempt great things for God."*

Again, my resolve was further strengthened as I saw in real life, the same picture, I had seen many times in my mind. At that moment, the Bible passage in Hebrews 11:1 made sense: *"Now faith is the substance of things hoped for, the evidence of things not seen."*

Reflection

"Your mission, if you decide to accept it, is an exciting, adventurous of abundant life with Almighty God as your very own personal guide in following His plan, on His terms, with His power."

— Dave Davidson

"God is not looking for nibblers of the possible, but for grabbers of the impossible."

— C.T. Studd.

"As we dare to step out of our comfort zones in pursuit of our God-given purposes, the resources of heaven become accessible to us."

— Unknown

CHAPTER NINE

An Adventure Of A Lifetime

"A ship in the harbor is safe, but that is not what ships are built for."

— John A. Shedd

The pursuit of our place in this world is a journey best travelled with the Shepherd of our souls who knows what we're made of, and the way we need to go. As I pursued this mission adventure, in my heart was the deep-seated understanding that my Father God is good, cares about me, and wants to be my guide to do His purpose for His glory and kingdom. Not long after the interview, I was informed that I had been accepted to participate in the Short-Term Exposure Program (STEP).

By this time, I had about 2 months to raise the required US$500 financial support necessary to cover the two months program and my transport money. Up to that point in my life, I had never seen US dollars before. I could not imagine how I would raise such a large amount of money. I didn't even know how I could explain to anyone I knew, that I wanted to go to Ghana for a mission trip and would need to pay someone US$500 to be able to do so. The thought of having to pay my support to be part of an international mission is still a strange concept to my people. The people I shared my plans with were initially supportive until they heard the part that I needed to raise about 100,000 Naira for my support. That amount of money was way too much for me to raise from anywhere I knew at the time. All I could do was to completely trust in God's provision and prepare the best I could. This was another dimension of learning to live by faith.

The Provision

In the middle of the uphill task of raising the financial support for the STEP program, I felt a sense of peace and hope that assured me God was in control. In reality, I started to count down the days to the deadline and still have no idea how God was going to provide the money I needed. Then finally, it was the day I was supposed to head out to Ghana to join the team for the mission adventure. Meanwhile, the day before, God had touched a friend of mine, Chukwudi, to support me with 15,000 Naira. This was a significant amount of money for him and me. He was only an apprentice at that time. As small as his donation was in relation to the needed 100,000, it was the boost I needed and, indeed, the seed necessary for me to step out. As a matter of fact, that was all I was able to raise for this trip.

On that Monday morning when I was supposed to travel to Ghana, I had a choice to make between the tyranny of the obvious and the triumph of faith. None of these choices are without consequences. In retrospect, I cannot imagine what life would have been for me now had I chosen to give up at that point in this pursuit. I would have missed the opportunity of experiencing God's provision, had I not stepped out in faith. Every step of faith we take in pursuit of God and His plan for our lives unlocks the miracles of His divine provision. Usually, this does not happen on our terms, but you can always count on the faithfulness and the goodness of God. Our lives are certainly testimonies in the making as we dare to go all the way with Jesus.

In the words of A.T Pierson: *"Our hour is unprecedented; our jungle is uncharted, and our opportunities are unmatched"* as we step out in faith on the journey God leads. God is waiting for us on the other side of our fears. The decision to step out in faith came after a careful consideration of the alternative. I was not sure what was going to happen on the other side in Ghana, since I had not met the financial requirements for participation in the STEP program.

As I arrived again at the ship in Ghana, prepared for the adventure, my heart beat faster and faster as the thought of being sent back raced through my mind because of my financial situation. At the foot of the gangway to the ship, I was warmly welcomed by some of the crew members and directed to the STEP coordinator who was visibly happy that I was able to make it eventually. I was somewhat encouraged by the warm welcome and hoped that the attitude would remain the same after discussing my financial challenges.

I didn't waste any time to tell the coordinator about the state of my finances, so they could decide my fate upfront. To my amazement, the optimism, smiles, and joy with which I was welcomed onboard on my arrival, were still visibly thereafter they heard of my financial situation. Their acceptance of me didn't change any bit by my story of lack of financial support. On the contrary, the coordinator encouraged me to settle in and assured me that we will continue to pray for God's provision and see how He would help us work through that. For a moment, I could not believe how calm and gracious anyone could be about the situation. For me, the best part was that I now had someone else working and praying with me for God's provision.

It felt really good just to know that God's got this. On one occasion, I particularly felt a strong sense of God's presence as the other STEP participants from around the world stood with me in prayers for God's financial provision. A few weeks later, I was informed by the STEP coordinator that someone visited the ship's bookshop and asked if there were specific needs that he could help with. My need for support was raised, and he contributed to that. Somehow, Jehovah Jireh did it again. I could now relax and fully participate in the STEP program without worrying about my support.

Cabin 270

The experiences of those two months become a precursor for what was going to be another two life-changing years in my life's journey, about five years later. Getting to build relationships with the other STEP participants was among the highlights of that adventure. Much of this friendship building happened in the large cabin 270 located in the front part of the ship, where most of the single male participants were housed.

There was never a dull moment in cabin 270. All sorts of personalities including some loud ones kept the atmosphere lively and friendly. I learned a lot about other countries and cultures as much as they learned about me and my culture.

If felt good to know that people from around the world would be keen to learn about me and my culture. That was the pinnacle of my life exposure. Still struggling with an inferiority complex to some extent, I tried to mind my business as much as possible and avoided being in the spotlight. A lot of things were very new to me – from food to equipment. Even such things as common as telephones were not something I was used to. I would rather take the pain and physically go to the other side of the ship to deliver a simple message, than pick up the phone in the cabin to talk because I was not sure how it worked. I had no intention of embarrassing myself trying or asking anyone what to do as that would have exposed my ignorance.

Unfortunately, it was not long before some of my cabin mates started wondering why I didn't use the phone. I remember one of the guys saying in a friendly but sarcastic tone: "Richard, the reason the telephone was invented is to save you the stress of having to go all the way to the other side of the ship just to say hello." We all laughed at the gesture, but he was gracious enough to explain to me how it works. This was one of the many basic things I had to get my head around in this new place.

At the end of that adventure, something shifted for the better in my life. My perception of who I was in relation to the people I considered the upper class of the society was changing for the better. I was beginning to see the fall of the wall of class distinction, that had locked me into always thinking of myself as a poor village boy without a father. I could now see beyond my limitations and things in my past that made me feel sorry for myself, to a future as bright as the promises of God. I came back to Nigeria in early January of 2002 with a transformed mindset and renewed understanding that there's nothing impossible for God to do. Back in school, my relationship with my mates was given a major boost.

Second Missionary Adventure

In 2006, four years after this life-changing experience, I was ready for another adventure onboard the MV Doulos, after completing my biochemistry degree program at the Federal University of Technology Owerri. This time, it was on a bigger scale and of course, more demanding with greater challenges, especially regarding raising the required US$300 monthly support to be on board for 2 years. As challenging as this was, it was nothing like the challenge I faced in my first adventure. I guess I had learned a thing or two about God's faithfulness in making provision for a vision centred on Him.

Just in the nick of time, God showed up to provide financial support from two of my STEP friends. My dear friend Robert from Australia and Marga from the Netherlands both stood with me financially through the two years of adventure on board the Doulos. On this side of life, these faithful friends will have no idea the magnitude of the impact their labour of love and sacrifice made in my life and the lives of many more, until that great morning in eternity, beyond the shores of time at the foot of Jesus. These guys, by their sacrificial act of love and obedience to God, taught me something about the blessedness of giving our little for God's glory. I thank God at every remembrance of these faithful friends.

Immeasurably More

Once again, the dream of a mission adventure on the world stage was within reach. For the very first time in my life, I was on board an airplane heading to Singapore to join the rest of the MV Doulos crew for a two-year adventure of a lifetime. It felt like a dream sitting down as a passenger onboard that massive Lufthansa Airbus transiting in Frankfurt on the way to Singapore.

In about six years, I had seen God do what was practically impossible in my life. He did far above all that I could ever dream of or plan for. Up there in the air, my heart was saturated with gratitude to God, so much so that I could only voice out "Thank You Jesus; thank You, Jesus." As I reflected on my journey, I was overwhelmed with thanksgiving beyond words. The words of the apostle Paul in Ephesians 3:20 finally made sense, "Now *to Him who is able to do immeasurably more than all we ask or imagine.*" (NIV)

My Utmost for His Highest

In light of all that God has done for me, I believe He deserves my utmost – the best of me for His glory. In the words of Oswald Chambers, *"My utmost for His highest."* Just a little bit like Mary in John's account of John 12:3, *"Then Mary took about a pint of pure nard, an expensive perfume; she poured it on Jesus' feet and wiped His feet with her hair. And the house was filled with the fragrance of the perfume."*

I felt a deep love in my heart for God drawing me closer to Him than I had ever been before. Up there, over 35,000 feet above sea level, I felt the immense presence of God as I reflected on the journey and the adventure ahead of me.

Reflected on what total surrender to God would look like for me, I was reminded of something I saw a few days before, while I was watching a video message of the famous preacher Benny Hinn. One particular solemn moment in his message while he was praying with tears on his cheeks and there was absolute quietness in the audience. He spoke these words to the Lord, *"Lord, that day when I shall stand before You in eternity, all I want to do is to be able to look into Your precious eyes and tell You that I tried...I did all I knew how for Your glory."* At first, it sounded a bit arrogant, but again, I looked at the tears on his cheeks, and all I could see was a man who was intentional and deliberate about giving God his utmost for His Highest.

I thought God used Benny to put it into perspective for me. Right then, I knew exactly what I wanted to do with my life. I wanted to be intentional about my love and service to God today and every day of my life on earth, with my eyes on eternity, and with the expectation of looking into His loving eyes one of these days with the courage to tell Him that "I tried. Lord, I was not lazy with Your grace in my life." Like Paul, I want to be able to say at the end of my journey, *"I have fought the good fight. I have finished my race. I have kept the faith."* (2 Timothy 4:7-8)

Richard Akubuiro

Reflection:

"If all were easy if all were bright, where would the cross be, and where the fight? But in the hardness, God gives to you chances of proving what He can do."

— Lucy Milward Booth-Hellberg

"Every step of Faith we take in pursuit of God and His plan for our lives unlocks the miracles of His divine provision."

— R. Akubuiro

CHAPTER TEN

Living Courageously

"Only one life, it will soon be past, only what's done for Christ will last."

— C.T. Studd

A few years ago, I noticed a strand of grey hair on my head and was quite fascinated looking at it. I did not give much thought to what that actually represents. Well, as the years passed by, I have continued to notice more and more of them. I think I get the message that all of those precious hair follicles are trying very hard to communicate to me. In case you haven't figured it out, with every birthday we celebrate something is growing older and the days and years of our lives are being lived. As easy as it is to slide through each day without much grip on the purpose of why we're here and what our lives are about, I think just sliding through day by day life is a very costly way to live. For one thing, I don't want to wake up one morning in a nursing home with my hairs all grey and my strength all gone without completing the thing God has put on my heart to do for His glory.

On the journey of life, God gives us precious moments and special people whose lives are like lighthouses and whose lights illuminate the path to find our way back to His purpose. I have certainly crossed the path of a number these people too numerous to mention. But for the sake of the subject of consideration here, the stories of three ordinary people stand out. The simplicity of their faith and their depth of commitment to what they believed about God's promises were both outstanding and contagious.

Living Courage

One of these men was one of my professors at the Federal University of Technology whose name I will shorten as Dr. Ogom. He was the dean of student affairs at the Federal University of Technology Owerri, during my undergraduate years. He has a strong physique and no- nonsense look that any right-minded student wouldn't dare mess with. What was even more interesting about Dr. Ogom, was his courage. He lived over 20 kilometres away from FUTO students' hostels, but whenever there was an issue in the hostels, irrespective of the time, he would be right there to address the situation. As the dean of the student affairs, he had access to security agents, especially because of the very dangerous terrain you had to drive through to get into the campus at night time. Under the cover of darkness, some of these places are known to be the hide-outs for students' cult initiations and other diabolic activities by the various cult groups.

Dr. Ogom never needed any police or security escort to travel through these dangerous roads to school, even at the worst time of the night. It was not long before the students became increasingly curious about his unusual courage and boldness. Several cult groups and their leaders became even more afraid of him, as they concluded he belonged to some more dangerous cult group.

I got to meet Dr. Ogom in 2002 when I was the president of the Student Christian Movement at FUTO. We met with him concerning matters affecting the welfare of the students, but I got to know him personally in 2003 when I became the President of the Joint Christian Campus Fellowship in FUTO. I worked with him to organize the anti-cult campaign for the university in 2003. I soon realized that Dr. Ogom was a very committed Christian. As I got to know more about him, one day I decided to ask him if he knew what students thought and said about him. He responded that he knew that all too well. Then came my next question as you could rightly guess.

I was keen to hear from him what was the secret to his exceptional courageous living. I wanted to hear what he knew about God that could generate such a courageous lifestyle. I still remember having a couple of student leaders with me at the time of this meeting with Dr. Ogom. I could see the keen faces of my friends who could not wait to hear his response. I guess some of us were expecting some philosophical or theological responses from him. But the simplicity and authenticity of his answer impacted my understanding of God and His purpose in the reality of daily living, as we simply seek to daily walk with Him in faith.

His answer was simple but profound. "I believe God when He said that life is a gift from Him, and as a gift from God, nobody has the power to take it from me without God's approval." Those words were authentic and a real-life commentary of the sermon on trusting God. I have heard sermons many times on this subject, but nothing made more sense to me as having a personal encounter with a simple man who dared to believe what God said and staked his entire life on it.

I saw how much difference it could make between talking about God's promises in His Word and actually believing it enough, to act on it accordingly. It sounded to me like that little "extra" step of taking God's Word seriously and acting on it, could mean the differencebetween an ordinary life and an extraordinary one. The lesson was as clear to me as it could be, and the choice was up to me, to be religious about God's Word and promises, or take them seriously and act on them as the truth they are. I left there with this question: "What would I do differently if I truly do not doubt in my heart that God would do what He said He would do?"

Inspiring Courage

To some of us who are slow learners, God gives as many learning opportunities as possible. Sometimes, He may go out of His way to offer some of those rare moments when He brings the lesson close to home. For me, the lesson does not get as close to home as the courageous display of trust in God's Word my wife expressed just before we got married.

One of the unusual tools God used to strengthen the relationship between my wife Tracey and I while we were still dating, was the long geographical distances between where I was in Papua New Guinea and where she was in

Albania. About two years after our first meeting in Brisbane on the Doulos ship in 2008, that beautiful girl was just about to become my wife. One of her requirements before she became my wife was to travel to Nigeria to meet my family and get used to our way of life in Nigeria. Fully persuaded in her heart, she was set to fly to Nigeria from Albania by herself. Deeply concerned about her safety while she was in Nigeria, five weeks before I was due to join her, I tried to get her to delay the plans, so at least I would be there to make sure she was safe. But Tracey was confident that God would keep her safe. Her trust in God's faithfulness and His ability to look after her even when she was the only white-skinned person in an African village was outstanding.

This was about the time when Nigeria was dealing with an epidemic of kidnappings. Whenever I thought of the reality of the risks we were up against, it caused me grave concern. What could I do from over 15,000 km away than to pray and trust God? At some point, I had to stop myself and look again at what I said I believed about God's faithfulness and ability to keep us safe according to His promises. Again, I saw in my wife a living testimony of true trust in God's faithful promises to look after His own.

Subsequently, I came around to truly trust God's faithfulness to take care of her. And He did. God faithfully protected her. This measure of trust and dependence on God's faithfulness to keep what is committed to Him leaves no question about the authenticity and the simplicity of faith in God that I know so little about. Over the years, my wife has continued to display this measure of trust in God that has always encouraged and stirred up my faith in Him.

A Crown Laid Down at His Feet

When I read the stories of the heroes of faith and outstanding individuals who did special acts to positively impact their generation, their experiences seem far removed. But as I read about some of these people, all I could see that they did differently was to give God their best. Doing what they could for His glory. They did what they could. They lived just as we're living today, but more than that, they chose to truly live. They gave life their best shot and lived for so much more.

"She did what she could" (Mark 14:8). Those were the words of our Lord Jesus as He spoke up in defence of Mary when the crowd criticized her actions. They had accused her of being wasteful as she broke her alabaster box of oil and rubbed it on His feet. For

Mary to make the difference in that season, it took that very alabaster box that belonged to her. That box had been in her possession perhaps for many years. But then came that moment of inspiration when she made the life-changing decision to give her utmost for His Highest. The beauty of that moment was that her critics could accuse her of wastage, but the freshness of the fragrance they could breathe in was undeniable. That extravagant act of worship left no question in the mind of everyone present of the depth of the love of God in her heart.

For some reason, this story about Mary and the alabaster box reminds me of one of the highlights of my experience in Papua New

Guinea, during my two years of work there. I happened to cross paths with a man who has left a significant impact on my life by the depth of his commitment to his calling. Pastor J. Kingal was a well-known and respected evangelist in PNG. His passion for God was exceptional. I would normally listen to his messages on the local radio station. In September of 2010, he held a one- month long evangelistic outreach event. I had never seen an evangelistic campaign as intensive as that. I have been involved in organizing outreaches and evangelistic campaigns, but this is the longest one I could ever imagine. I looked forward to tuning in to the local radio station every day for the event. The level of commitment and sacrifice involved, as well as the spiritual impact in the nation of Papua New Guinea during that one month of constant intercession and outreach, can only be unravelled in eternity.

There is no doubt Pastor Kingal gave his best shot to his compelling vision, to reach out to his nation PNG. He did what he could. Sadly, this event was one of his last before he was called home to heaven a few weeks after the outreach.

The accident that led to his death shocked the entire nation. My heart was so broken to hear the sad story of the death of this hero of faith. But I know he gave the Master all he had and did what he could while he had the chance. At his funeral service, I could not hold back the tears as I thought of how short our mission here on earth could be. We have no clue what the future holds. All I could think about was to plead with God to help me do what I could for His glory, while I still can.

Reflection

"God does not begin by asking us about our ability, but only about our availability, and if we then prove our dependability, he will increase our capability."

Richard Akubuiro

— Neal A. Maxwell

"You can give without loving, but you cannot love without giving."

— Amy Carmichael

"Night is coming when no one can work"

— (John 9:4).

Let Hope Arise

Recently, I had a conversation with an elderly man who has had his fair share of life challenges. He has lived through a lot of experiences where he lost family members, his home, and treasured possessions. As I sat and listened to his stories, the thought of my losses raced through my mind. For me, in the middle of those experiences of loss, hope has continued to stand out as the anchor for my soul through the challenging seasons of life.

In January 2002, I had the painful experience of losing my mother. In the few days leading up to her death as she lay in the hospital bed in the neighbouring town, all I could do was pray and plead with God not to take her away yet. She was my whole world. I could not imagine life without her. All my life, I had longed for the privilege of giving back to the woman who had given everything she had to look after me and my siblings. As she grew weaker and weaker, I could not stand the sight of watching her go. I was seriously worried about how I would cope if God chose to take her home. My other siblings were very concerned about me because they knew how much Mum meant to me. It was not until she finally passed away that God brought me into the real meaning of the power of hope.

I will never forget that moment amid my grief when God spoke to my heart in the words of John 14:18, *"I will not leave you as orphans."* This was one of those unexplainable moments when God shifts something in the very inside of your being for good. From that moment, God has shown incredible faithfulness to me in comforting my grieving heart. He has looked after me and has exchanged the spirit of heaviness for his garment of praise. And through that grief process has granted me a glimpse into the experiences of hurting people around me, and the grace to share His love and compassion with them.

> *"Blessed be the God and Father of our Lord Jesus Christ, the Father of mercies and God of all comfort, who comforts us in all our tribulation, that we may be able to comfort those who are in any trouble, with the comfort with which we ourselves are comforted by God."*
>
> **(2 Corinthians 1:3-4)**

For many poor and vulnerable people in the villages around the world, this comfort comes to them in the form of hope. The hope for a better future for their children. The hope for the opportunities to fulfil their dreams. The hope for the provision of the basic needs of their families, and the ultimate hope of eternal future in the presence of God beyond this life. It is this hope that provides an anchor for our souls. Let hope arise!

In some form or shape, I want to be an agent of hope to many of those orphans and poor children who cannot go to school. An active participant in the hope movement, reaching out for thousands of unemployed graduates in Nigeria and around the world. A channel of hope to widows and vulnerable people groups who cannot fight for themselves, and a voice of hope for the poor children living with disabilities in the slums of Africa without any form of government support. Let hope arise!

This message of hope underpins the vision of the Gospel Foundation International (GFI). There are millions of children around the world going to bed every day without food and anyone looking out for them. The Nigerian Bureau of Statistics in 2004 said over 60.9% of Nigerians were living in absolute poverty. That is over 100 million people living on less than $1 a day. That is not right!

It's not enough to just talk about it. We can be a part of the solution. You and I can make the difference. We can start from somewhere. That is what the GFI Legacy Project is about. GFI Legacy Project is the continuation of the legacy of my parents in their outreach to the poor and the vulnerable members of our communities.

Richard Akubuiro

The Summary of the Vision of the Gospel Foundation International

Legacy Project

When we think about the overwhelming challenges and the odds against the effort to improve the quality of life for poor and vulnerable members of our societies, much of what comes to our minds is a list of what we cannot do. But how about the things we can do? What about the capacities and capabilities within our grasps that can make the difference? How about the wealth of talents and dreams God has planted in our hearts? What about the potential and possibilities in the forms of brilliant human capital in our nations? What about the millions of hectares of farmlands with the potential to transform Nigeria and the other African nations into the food baskets of Africa and the world?

Faced with the insurmountable challenge of leading the children of Israel across the Red Sea into their Promised Land, Moses cried out to God for help. As an answer to his cry, God turned Moses' attention to what was in his

hands. *"What is in your hands."* (Exodus 4:20) For Moses, it was '*a shepherd's rod.*' The question for us today is, what is your '*shepherd's rod*'?

For the little boy in the story of Jesus feeding the five thousand people, his 'shepherd's rod' was his five small barley loaves and two small fish, which he was willing to give to Jesus. "There is a lad here who has five barley loaves and two small fish, but what are they among so many?" (John 6:9)

Overall Objective:

The Legacy Project is a two-fold community- focused education and sustainable agricultural initiative. The Education initiative seeks to build the capacity of vulnerable children in the proposed rural communities by providing them with an early childhood educational foundation for a better future, through the establishment of community schools in the local areas hosting the Agricultural project.

The sustainable agriculture project seeks to implement an integrated agricultural model, that will contribute to food security and seek to provide employment to 1000 local poor people over the first 10 years. This project will support youth agricultural entrepreneurship and build the capacity of local farmers, to engage in productive and sustainable agricultural practices in their community. The Project will develop an integrated and innovative strategies that will practically demonstrate the good news of God's love through capacity building and the provision of employment to the poor and vulnerable members of the local host communities.

This project will be implemented in a rural farming community of the South-eastern Nigeria and will be a model that will be replicated in the other sites as God opens the door.

Strategy:

This is an innovative and integrated agricultural venture that will optimize the natural resources of 50,000 hectares of farmland and transform it into a sustainable agricultural and horticultural business hub.

Project Operation Approach:

The Project operations will be guided by a God- centred and stewardship-based approach, that is built on a commitment to environmental sustainability, social responsibility, and economic self-sustainability. is built on a commitment to environmental sustainability, social responsibility, and economic self-sustainability.

I believe that together, we can be that "Isaiah 58:12 generation" who will rebuild the waste places and restore hope where it's most needed. As a generation, we can cause hope to arise for millions of poor and vulnerable people in the South-eastern Nigeria and around the world, who are living in poverty, with the little resources God has put in our hands.

Isaiah 58:12 *"Those from among you shall build the old waste places; You shall rise up the foundations of many generations; And you shall be called the Repairer of the Breach, The Restorer of Streets to Dwell In."*

This book is a seed towards this Legacy Project and all the proceeds from it will go towards the project.

You can get the full version of the vision GFI Legacy Project by contacting me at **gospelfoundationinternational@gmail.com.**

www.ingramcontent.com/pod-product-compliance
Lightning Source LLC
Chambersburg PA
CBHW032042290426
44110CB00012B/913